I Am Human:

Food for the Archons

Humanities Psychic Connection,
Simulated Realities, Parallel Worlds, and
the Manipulation of Mankind

Dennis Nappi II

Published by Service of Change, LLC
© 2019 Dennis Nappi II

Cover Artwork by Aimee Wright

ISBN: 978 0 9911375 9 6

Contents

Part 3: Manipulation of the Holy Spirit

For you, Dad. I will never give up. I will never forget. This is not over yet, and somehow, someway, I will find an answer - in this life or the next!

We, those whom you see here, are, then, the avengers of the torments and suffering of our fathers.

Oj K'u paq'ol re wa'e ki ra'il, Ki k axk'ol ri qa qajaw.

~Mayan Popol Vuh

Death

As I watched my father convulse helplessly during his final seizure, a terrifying realization overcame me. It was not observed with my eyes, but felt throughout my body, as he lay there, shaking - dying. It was killing my father, and we stood there watching him suffering in pain, wasting away to a frail, confused-fragment of what he once was. When he stopped shaking, there was a moment of silence, and then the screaming started. He screamed for over an hour in pain, and we can only assume he was having yet another massive stroke. His breathing was labored, and he fought for each breath despite our requests for him to let go. He would not give up, but as the minutes dripped by like hours, I began to suspect that he was unable to do so. Something was keeping him alive, and after denying its existence for so long, my conscious mind finally started to accept the possibility of this presence. Although my father was the one being tortured, it was us that it wanted. Like an enemy sniper who painfully wounds a soldier in battle to draw the rest of the group into an ambush, my father lay as helpless bait while we were unknowingly pulled into an emotional trap. It wasn't our physical bodies that it wanted but our emotional output that it craved. With each scream of pain or gasp for air, our sadness grew heavier and more massive like a thick-energetic soup that flowed from our hearts just waiting for them to suck it down. It was then that I finally accepted a terrifying possibility: They are out there, just beyond our perception. They are always out there, and they have been for an incredibly long time, feeding on us and preying on our fears and emotions like a leach burrowed deeply in the cold dark shadows of our minds.

The Question

Most days I still find it hard to believe. I feel this knowing deep inside, yet my mind tries to convince me I'm crazy; that this is all in my head and I am living out some deep-rooted fantasy or suffering from the mental strain of a short-lived counterintelligence career. Nothing is what it seems, and so much of what I once believed was based on a carefully constructed lie. Am I simply enthralled by the latest conspiracy theories? Or is this real?

For as far back as I can remember I have struggled to grasp the true concept of reality and have found a great deal of confusion deciphering between my perceived reality and the tangibility of the dream world. It is most difficult to accept what I have come to realize when I embrace the warmth of the sun on a calm summer day, or when I gaze at the beauty of the snow glistening in the morning light on a brisk winter morning. How can I be a victim of such cruelty? How is it that we are all victims of the same cruel force, yet no one seems to know about it?

My perception seems too far-fetched to be true. I must be insane for even considering the possibility, yet I can't shake the notion that this is real. It has always been real, and this knowing has been a driving force throughout my entire life. Although I am constantly searching for validation, I have realized that when I do receive it, my mind craves more and allows doubt to creep back once again. But this is very real, and I have sampled that reality on countless occasions throughout my life. I have heard Nature's voice as I sat quietly in her presence; I have experienced communication with something greater than my perception of self; and I have been visited by *them*. They are the ones who come in the night, who offer both terror and anguish. They bring with them a paralyzing fear and a silent control that has humbled even my bravest attempts at resistance. They have infected my life from the comfort of the deep dark shadows in which they hide, and I suspect they have always been there: waiting, watching, and manipulating our lives.

I have come to believe their intentions are detrimental to our potential, yet I am thankful for my encounters with them. For without them, I would not know them, and without knowing them, I would not question. It is our ability to question that drives this quest because a question can force us to dissect even the most unsuspicious falsehood on a journey toward truth. It is through *them* that I have formulated my question of resistance, and it is through my resistance that I have developed more questions. So, as I invite you on this journey through my experiences, I will pose a simple question for you to ponder as you read. Consider its value in understanding, and the insight such an understanding can offer. Be aware, however, that searching for an answer to this question will most likely start an antagonizing reflection of self, society, humanity, and our greater purpose. Some of the information you uncover on this journey may be painful to bear and life changing, but I implore you to push on; for to ignore the answer to this question is to live in ignorance of this threat! It is far older than the footprint of humanity, and it has been waiting, watching, and preying on us. Not knowing this threat leaves us defenseless against it and may very well cost us our lives and quite possibly our souls. Finding the answer to this question will result in our liberation from a cunning predator.

So, this question I pose is quite simple, yet massively complex. Use care in exploring it, and take time to do so because it may just save your life and the lives of the ones you love:

Who are we?

Part 1: The 6th Sense

In the country of Gad'a-renes, after Jesus freed a man from his possession by unclean spirits, Jai'rus, one of the rulers of the synagogue, approached him. Jai'rus fell to Jesus's feet and begged him to save his daughter, who was close to death.

Jesus agreed, and as he made his way through the town, a crowd followed behind him. Within that crowd was a sick woman. For twelve years she suffered from a blood condition and despite visiting many physicians and after spending all of her money, she could not be cured. As Jesus walked through town, she joined the crowd and pressed in behind him. The woman reached out and touched his clothes, believing that touching him would heal her sickness, and in doing so the plague dried up from her blood and she was made well. As this happened, Jesus felt his virtue flowing from him, turned around, and asked: "Who touched my clothes?" (Mark 5: 25-30)

How did he know? What did Jesus experience that allowed him to recognize someone siphoning his healing energy? Furthermore, how did the sick woman know that touching Jesus would heal her? What exactly was the "virtue" that she took from Jesus?

Communication

On a particularly hot day in July of 2009, I found myself escaping to the cool air of my local bookstore. I was searching for my next reading adventure, hopeful that I would find some answers to the incessant question that continually plagued my thoughts. I wandered curiously down aisle after aisle, searching the occult, spiritual, and religious sections while visualizing my intuition leading me to that glowing book with all the answers I had ever hoped to find.

To my disappointment, the magic book of answers never manifested and I found myself staring at the same rows of muted books as I looped through the same three aisles. On one of my passes, I noticed a man, probably in his early thirties, standing at the end of one of the rows. He was dressed appropriately for the weather and area, and didn't seem out of place in the least. Everything about this man's physical appearance seemed normal. However, as I approached him I felt a growing discomfort press at the base of my neck. It was a deep pressure that alerted me as if something dangerous was pursuing me. As I walked closer to this man, the pressure grew in intensity. I passed him, and walked quickly to another aisle. I gave myself a moment to explore the feelings I was experiencing, and realized I had a sense that this casual-looking man was following me. Furthermore, I sensed he somehow knew I had detected his presence. A few moments later, he came around the aisle and walked toward me, just as I had expected him to. He passed uncomfortably close behind me, almost touching me, undoubtedly violating my personal space and causing my anxiety to spike. As he passed, the pressure at the base of my neck increased in intensity and I then felt what can best be described as a draining of my energy. It seemed to be flowing out of me in his direction as he passed, as if someone had opened a valve and allowed it to drain freely. I immediately glared at him, making eye contact briefly before I rushed out of the store to the safety of my vehicle. Once there, the draining sensation stopped, and the pressure at the base of my neck subsided.

As I got in my car and drove toward home, the words "psychic vampire" floated through my mind. I had previously read an article that talked about these people who have an ability to psychically drain energy from their victims. But were they actually real? Had I really encountered one? The realness of the interaction was difficult for me to deny, yet I still tried to attribute what I had experienced to an overactive imagination. I am aware that the mind can sometimes trick the body into feeling various sensations, but in this instance the sensations I had were not in any way preceded by thoughts of psychic vampirism (or anything similar). Everything was spontaneous. Over the years, I have learned to interpret my intuitive perceptions by judging them based on the immediate feelings I get prior to my conscious mind's contamination. In this instance, my perception of him attempting to drain me was raw and untainted by my damaging conscious thoughts.

But had this encounter really happened? Was the casual-looking man in the bookstore actually trying to siphon my energy? In analyzing this brief encounter, a few observations came to mind. Assuming this was a real event, I perceived the following:

I felt his intent. It was a pressure at the back of my neck, as if my fight or flight reaction was being stimulated and giving me a sense of being pursued. If an energy exchange was in fact pending, then this sensation was a possible indicator that it was happening. Was I feeling his presence, or simply detecting the drain on my own energy?

The next thing I observed about the encounter was my clear perception that he was aware that I knew what he was doing. If my perception was accurate, does this indicate a level of 2-way communication between us?

If this is true, then this is how our conversation went:

Him: "I'm going to take your energy."

Me: "Hey! I can hear you and I'm not going to let you."

Him: "I'm going to try to do it anyway."

Me: "Fuck you, I'm leaving."

Although not a single-audible word was uttered between us, this was the unspoken conversation that I perceived. The fact that I sensed he was going to follow me, and then moments later he walked uncomfortably close to me lends, in my opinion, some validation to what I was experiencing. If I am correct in my assumptions, then we have to wonder not only if human beings are capable of sending and receiving energy, but also if that energy is encoded with information. If that energy is encoded, are we then able to process and interpret that encoded data? Lastly, if we can receive and transmit data-encoded energy, can we also steal the energy of another, or send someone misleading information?

30 years ago, had we told people we would someday be able to stream video, images, text, and so much more into a small device that fits in our hands, the average person would have rolled their eyes and told us we watched too much Star Trek. Today, we enjoy instant communication through the wireless Internet – a system that takes data and transmits it invisibly through the air to a device that is able to receive, interpret, and

respond to such data. A mobile device, however, is much different than a living, breathing-human being. Or is it?

Do humans possess a mechanism by which to transmit and receive data? Surely people with documented psychic abilities must have a mechanism that allows them to access the desired information. If this is the case, do we have evidence of it? Such a concept was clearly discussed in Mark 5, as the woman intended to siphon Jesus's energy. When she did, Jesus knew, much like when this man seemingly drained me of my energy, I also knew. This observation is by no means meant to compare me to Jesus. It does suggest, however, that humans may be capable of energetic transference and communication.

The 6th Sense Organ

Author, experiencer, and researcher Whitley Strieber has been a pioneer in exploring, documenting, and sharing his experiences with what has come to be known as the abduction phenomenon. In 1987, he shocked the world when he released *Communion*, which detailed his encounters with small, large-eyed creatures that kidnapped him in the night to conduct torturous experiments on him. After *Communion*, Strieber's experiences continued, and so did his reporting of them.

Late one evening while staying in a hotel during a book tour, Strieber reports the arrival of a strange visitor. He was never able to identify this person, but he seemed to possess great knowledge about the human condition, metaphysics, and our role in this universe.

In his book *The Key, A True Encounter,* Strieber recounts his powerful conversation with this mysterious late-night visitor, some of which is relevant to our current exploration into the conscious transfer of human energy. During their discussion, Strieber asked his visitor: "What are Psychics?"

The visitor responded:

"A part of the electromagnetic field that fills the nervous system rests a few centimeters above the skin, outside of the body. This field is an organ just like the heart or the brain. It is in quantum superposition, the electrons effectively everywhere in the universe and nowhere specific. It may be imprinted by information from anywhere and any time. With it, you may see other worlds, you may see the past and the future, you may see into the lives of those around you. You may haunt God..."[1]

What Strieber's visitor revealed was a possible mechanism by which psychic communication was possible. In addition, the mysterious visitor explained that through practice, people can learn to better control this electromagnetic organ.

---

[1] Strieber, Whitley. (2011) *The Key: A True Encounter*. J.P. Tarcher/Penguin (pp.54)

8

Was I unknowingly using this organ to communicate with the man in the bookstore? If so, could I learn to activate it at will? If this organ exists, does it allow for the siphoning of energy from another? Is this the mechanism by which Jesus was aware of the woman's siphoning of his own virtue?

Strieber's visitor did not supply any contact information, so to date nobody has been able to confirm the authenticity of his existence. However, if we can verify the validity of his statements, his identity may not be necessary at all.

Remote Viewing

In today's society, we experience life through the five-sense reality of taste, sound, smell, touch, and sight. If we can't detect something through those senses, we assume an object or phenomenon must not exist unless our technology can find a way to demonstrate that existence by presenting it in a reality that our senses can perceive. But what about those events that occur beyond the perception of our five senses and technology? How do we explain a dream that comes true, or an intuitive "gut feeling" that helps us make the correct choice? How do we explain when we correctly guess who is calling on the phone without looking at the caller ID? When such events happen, are they just random acts of luck? Or are we experiencing a form of psychic communication through a wireless-psychic network? Are these events mere glimpses of our potential to "see" and know things? With so many incidents of psychic phenomenon, why do we insist on working so hard to disprove their existence instead of trying everything in our power to understand and utilize them?

Despite documented events, verified psychic observations, and witness & participant testimony, when we start talking about psychic phenomenon, the average person tends to diminish the credibility of this information, even when presented with verifiable scientific data. People may have a general interest in these accounts for the entertainment value they offer at social gatherings, but to accept them as fact would risk being labeled as crazy or weird. In addition, the person sharing psychic information may lose credibility in the face of his audience if he seems to believe in this "stuff" too much. Now add a classified government psychic-spying program that was later used to uncover the presence of extraterrestrial life forms on Earth, and you have one hell of a conspiracy theory that even most conspiracy theorists won't want to touch.

But what if a method was developed to verify the existence of psychic phenomenon and that method could be used to collect data on any subject, time, event, or location in existence? If you, the reader, were able to review such data, would it change your mind? Would it change your world-view? Would it change your life and relationship to the world around you? Or would you continue to search for a way to discredit this life-changing discovery?

History

In the 1970s, a procedure known as Remote viewing was developed through the Stanford Research Institute (SRI), and funded by the Central Intelligence Agency for almost 20 years. A simple Internet search will yield hours of video testimony by founders Russel Targ and Harold (Hal) Puthoff, about their findings and successes. They tell fantastic stories of their work with Ingo Swann, an incredibly gifted natural psychic, and others, and explain that their research demonstrated that people without any previous psychic experience were quickly able to learn to be quite talented remote viewers. In an article published by Puthoff and Targ in the *Proceedings of the IEEE* in March of 1976, it states that:

"persons such as visiting scientists and contract

monitors, with no previous exposure to such concepts (as remote viewing), have learned to perform well; and subjects who have trained over a one-year period have performed excellently under a variety of experimental conditions. Our accumulated data thus indicate that both specially selected and unselected persons can be assisted in developing remote perceptual abilities up to a level of useful information transfer."[2]

The article goes onto explain that: *"In experiments of this type, we have three principal findings. First, we have established that it is possible to obtain significant amounts of accurate descriptive information about remote locations. Second, an increase in the distance from a few meters up to 4000 km separating the subject from the scene to be perceived does not in any apparent way degrade the quality or accuracy of perception. Finally, the use of Faraday cage electrical shielding does not prevent high-quality descriptions from being obtained."*[2]

In one of their referenced experiments, described as "a typical level of proficiency

---

[2] Puthoff, Harold E. and Targ, Russel, (1976, March 3)"A Perceptional Channel for Information Transfer over Kilometer Distances: Historical Perspective and Recent Research." *Proceedings of the IEEE,* Vol. (pp. 64 329 – 354) Retrieved from http://www.espresearch.com/espgeneral/Remote-Viewing-IEEE-1976.pdf

that can be reached and that we have come to expect in our research," they describe an experiment involving Hal Puthoff's trip to Costa Rica. Dr. Puthoff spent 10 days in Costa Rica and was assigned to keep detailed notes of his locations and activities, to include photographs of his specific targets at a specific time each day to be compared with remote viewing data upon his return. The remote viewers were told only that Dr. Puthoff was in Costa Rica and nothing more, and it was noted that none of the viewers had ever been to Costa Rica.

One viewer focused on Dr. Puthoff's activities on a particular day, and perceived a beach and an ocean setting with an airport on the beach. The viewer described a runway with the ocean at the end. The viewer knew Costa Rica was mostly mountainous, and assumed the data was incorrect, however, upon later inspection of Dr. Puthoff's photos, found his session to be accurate in detail of the airport, to include the beach, runway, and ocean at the end when compared to the photos. Since then, remote viewing has expanded in magnificent directions, exploring the past, the future, other planets, and even alien civilizations.

In 1996, Dr. Courtney Brown's book, *Cosmic Voyage, A Scientific Discovery of Extraterrestrials Visiting Earth*, was published. In his book, Dr. Brown explains that he was trained in remote viewing, and states that:

"(r)emote viewing is an exacting and demanding discipline that involves a precisely structured set of protocols, and only an individual who has been fully trained by a competent teacher can utilize it accurately for data-gathering purposes."[3]

Dr. Brown goes onto explain the procedure of "Scientific Remote Viewing," which was used by him to obtain the data for his book. At no point during his explanation did he reference crystal balls, tarot cards, or tealeaves. What Dr. Brown described was a specific set of protocols that take a remote viewer through multiple steps, followed in a specific fashion, in a specific order, to obtain the desired data. Typically, the only data given to the viewer is a set of coordinate numbers; in other words, the viewer has no idea what the target is that he will be observing. The coordinate numbers

---

[3] Brown, Courtney. (1996) Cosmic Voyage: a Scientific Discovery of Extraterrestrials Visiting Earth. Dutton. (pp. 16)

are assigned to the target, but the viewer knows only the numbers and nothing more. Once the numbers are read, the viewer begins his process of psychically collecting the data to obtain the desired information represented by the coordinates.

When the session is over, the data is reviewed and analyzed by comparing sketches, notes, impressions, and everything recorded by the viewer to the actual target to determine its validity and accuracy.

In one of his sessions labeled "Reality Check #1," Dr. Brown was assigned target coordinates for a verifiable target. He was being tasked to gather data that could easily be confirmed to test his accuracy. During the early part of his session, Dr. Brown described the basic textures, colors and backgrounds of his target, and as he moved through the remote viewing process, the data became a bit more complex. At one point, his monitor asked him to "(c)ue on the idea of 'activity.'"

Dr. Brown responded: *"OK. There are humans walking around here. They have clothes on, business clothes. There are suits, jackets, slacks, and both men and women. They are all wearing business attire. There is a desk in the room. It seems to have something like a blotter on it."*

"There is a man sitting at the desk. Wow! This is an important man."[3]

A few moments later, Dr. Brown states: "I am staring at President Clinton, straight in the face, as he sits at his desk."

The monitor then instructed Dr. Brown to stop the session and informed him that the target was "The Oval Office/White House, Washington D.C." Later in the book, Dr. Brown and his monitor conducted a second calibration session, where Dr. Brown correctly identified his target as the "Battle of Gettysburg." Both "reality checks" mentioned in his book lend strong credibility to the techniques being employed by Dr. Brown as a means of accurately gathering psychic data on verifiable targets. They offer tangible proof that with proper training, humans can learn to psychically view any time, world, or event they wish to "see."

Dr. Brown currently runs "The Farsight Institute," a non-profit organization located in Atlanta Georgia, where he oversees the training of new remote viewers. Through the Farsight Institute, Dr. Brown and his colleagues have conducted some fascinating remote viewing research and explorations, to include targets such as The Roswell Crash, 9/11, Area 51, The JFK Assassination, Adolf Hitler, and many more. In addition, Dr. Brown and his team are currently working on the "TimeCross Project" where each month, remote viewers predict the major news events for the upcoming month with a high degree of accuracy. The work coming out of the Farsight Institute is cutting edge, and represents hopeful potential in developing psychic abilities for the purposes of gathering accurate data. They even offer free training courses in remote viewing through their website, farsight.org. In referring back to Strieber's mysterious visitor's statements, it does seem that we are capable of enhancing our 6th sense abilities hence lending credibility to his statements of being able to improve our own psychic talents.

Out of the Body

One morning, when I was about 7-years old, I was lying comfortably in my bed fast asleep before school. The warmth of my bed enveloped me with the soft plushness of my blankets. The room was silent, and sunlight was just beginning to peek through my shades, slightly penetrating the darkness behind my eyelids. Then, the silence was broken as my mother's gentle voice floated in from my doorway.

"Dennis," she said. "It's time to wake up."

I sat up slowly and looked at her standing in my doorway.

"Dennis," she said.

I looked at her, puzzled. "What?" I said, tiredly.

"Dennis," she repeated. "It's time to wake up

for school."

"Mom, I'm up," I explained, but she didn't seem to notice.

"Dennis," her tone was still soft and almost soothing. "It's time to wake up."

"Mom! I'm up!" I said, but she continued to call my name when suddenly I found myself lying flat again with my eyes closed. I opened my eyes, sat up and there she was, standing in my doorway calling my name. Confused, I smiled up at her wondering why she hadn't seen me a moment before. This time, she stopped calling my name.

"I laid out your clothes. Get dressed and come down for breakfast," she said, and then went downstairs to finish with her morning routines.

One can easily argue that I dreamt my mother was standing in my doorway while she was calling my name. But this felt different than a dream. I saw her, just as she was, but she didn't see me until I woke up a second time. Is it possible that something else was at work here? As I grew older, I'd have similar experiences on occasion. I'd wake up; get out of my bed and go to leave my bedroom only to find my hand float right through the doorknob. Upon realizing this strangeness, I'd find myself back in my bed to repeat the process. Sometimes this would take several attempts before I'd actually be able to leave my room. It's as if I was unknowingly leaving my physical body and moving through my room in a different form.

Explorer Bob Monroe recounts his first experience as he awoke one morning to find himself floating on the ceiling, looking down at his body. Afraid he was going to die, he had multiple tests and evaluations performed, yet found he was in perfect health. At realizing he was not going to die, he began exploring this unique experience which opened up an incredible world of adventure and learning for him.

In all three of his books, Monroe describes his ability to leave his body at will to explore far-away worlds, distant times, or the room down the hall. In his third book, *Ultimate Journey*, Monroe explains:

"An out-of-body experience (OOBE) is a condition where you find yourself outside of your physical body, fully conscious, and able to perceive and act as if you were functioning physically –

with several exceptions. You can move through space (and time?) slowly or apparently somewhere beyond the speed of light. You can observe, participate in events, make willful decisions based upon what you perceive and do. You can move through physical matter such as walls, steel plates, concrete earth, oceans, air, even atomic radiation without effort or effect."[4]

Such a description certainly explains how I was able to see my mother that morning, yet she couldn't hear my responses. It also lends credibility to my hand passing right through the doorknob.

After he first left his body naturally in 1958, Monroe's research into the experience led to his development of HemiSynch technology where, through the use of tones played at different frequencies in each ear, can produce different states of consciousness and awareness. Monroe founded the Monroe Institute where training, research, and exploration into the study of consciousness and altered states of consciousness continue today. Thousands of people have attended the institute, where they are given a unique

---

[4] Monroe, Robert A. (1994) *Ultimate Journey*. Broadway Books.

opportunity to explore their own inner-selves as they gain a deeper understanding of consciousness and the potential of the human spirit. It's also interesting to note that in preparation for his training in Scientific Remote Viewing, Dr. Courtney Brown attended one of Monroe's training sessions. Brown also states that during the initial development of the military's remote viewing program:

"To introduce the general subject of altered awareness to trainees, the team was first sent to the Monroe Institute in Virginia, where they received formal training in out-of-body states."[3]

In comparing the verified and repeated results of scientific remote viewing along with the experience and research of Robert Monroe and the Monroe Institute, to the capabilities of the electromagnetic organ described by Streiber's visitor, the similarities are almost identical. If you recall, the visitor stated of the organ:

"It may be imprinted by information from anywhere and any time. With it, you may see other worlds, you may see the past and the future, you may see into the lives of those around you. You may haunt God..."[1]

Strieber's visitor also stated we can learn to control this organ. Is remote viewing or Monroe's OOBEs a result of the development of this organ? Had Dr. Brown's training allowed him to activate it so he could gather psychic data? Does this organ grow stronger through the training sessions offered at the Monroe Institute? Both approaches offer repeated results with verifiable targets that demonstrate the potential for anyone to learn how to develop this ability. They offer the proof that so many people demand yet refuse to review. One would expect an incredible breakthrough like this to top every headline and be taught in every school. But our news media omits these findings, and our schools are unaware of this potential. Why?

With an ability to tap into psychic data, we would be able to make better decisions and prepare for our future. Natural disasters could be predicted. Wars could be avoided. Disease could be identified and prevented and lives could be saved. With such a tool as readily available as our senses of taste, touch, sound, sight, and feel, we could revolutionize the way we interact with the world and potentially improve the human condition for everyone. Such an ability, it would seem, would empower mankind and limit our level of dependency on government to make choices on our behalf. It would also force a level of transparency since the ability to keep secrets would most-likely be eliminated from our society.

This potential does exist, and it exists in all of us. We have the power to use this tool, but until we open ourselves to this potential, it will sit dormant in a state of atrophy, while the world falls apart around us. When examining this situation, one has to wonder why those charged with leadership over the world's people would want to deny the existence of this power, knowing full well the consequences of this denial could mean more suffering, conflict and death throughout the world.

Communion With Nature

In the summer of 2010, I spent a lot of time meditating, as I was trying to reach out and explore the capabilities and limits of my intuition. I took a strong interest in nature and tried my best to connect with her through my daily meditation sessions. That summer, I found nature to be one of my greatest teachers. I took a strong interest in power animals and nature spirits, and in my sessions, I would try to reach out psychically to see if I could befriend a guide to lead me through my meditations. I had some success with beautiful visions of wild animals approaching me and sitting in front of me. I felt thankful in their acknowledgments of my calls to them, but still wanted something more tangible; something to prove this was more than just my imagination.

A few days a week, I would take a bike ride to a business park near my home. It was virtually empty and set on a beautifully wooded lot. I'd casually ride my bike down each of the quiet winding roadways and take in the beauty of the lush-green surrounding woods. After a few trips, I began stopping behind a particular building. In the tree line beyond the building, there was a quiet trail that led into the woods and crossed a small trickling stream. Each time I would get to that spot, I'd get off of my bike and spend a few moments meditating, getting lost in the soft trickle of water flowing through the woodlands before me. The world was still around me, as the warm summer sun enveloped me to the sounds of birds singing joyfully in the trees. I usually focused on some of the challenges I was facing that week and asked for the strength and wisdom to continue. I'd then get back on my bike and continue my ride through the park.

After my first meditation in that spot, I rode my bike to the edge of the park. It was the last area to explore before I had to turn around and go home. There was a concrete divider where the road ended, and the thick deciduous forest began. Bits of trash were strewn about the ground, along with a small stack of forgotten and weathered wooden pallets lying among the thick overgrowth of weeds. Spiny thorn bushes grew heavily at the end of the road, as if to completely block entry into the forest from my vantage. I stopped my bike and sat there for a moment, reflecting on my meditation, and asked for a sign that the connection I was feeling was something real. I wanted to have proof that nature was hearing my meditations, and that I was not alone.

In the middle of my thought, I heard a feint rustling sound. The leaves on the ground in front of me were crunching gently, as if something was moving over them. I glanced down, and at first saw nothing. But then there was movement - something dark sliding through the leaves. I looked closer, and saw a large black snake casually making its way back into the forest. It seemed as if it wanted me to see it, like it had been sitting there waiting for my arrival before returning to the safety of the forest. The blackness of this magnificent creature caught the fading sunlight and its scales glistened as it moved. It was one of the biggest snakes I had ever seen in the wild, easily 3 feet long. I watched it until it disappeared into the thick weeds beneath the thorn bushes, and then all went silent as the sunlight continued to fade.

In my 5 years living in that area, I had never before encountered any snakes, let alone one 3-feet long. Was this my sign from Nature that she heard me? Was I experiencing a connection? If this was the case, I felt immediately terrified that she chose a snake as my messenger. Memories from my Catholic upbringing flashed through my mind. The Devil tempted Eve with the forbidden fruit in the form of a serpent. Had I just had communion with the Prince of Darkness? Was this new spiritual path I was following leading me to Hell? Or was there something more? Despite my fears over the potential significance of this encounter, I felt a growing sense of excitement at the possibility that I had made contact. Nature had spoken to me, and although she didn't speak in audible words, she had shown me she was listening.

Once I arrived home, I started searching the

Internet for the significance of snakes in spiritual encounters. To my surprise, snakes represented something far different than the satanic images my Catholic training had instilled in me. At the very top of my search results, I came across a website called "Shamanic Journeys," which had lists of just about every power animal and their significance. Although the original article has since been taken down, an updated version dated February 2015 written by the same author, Ina Woolcott, was available at the time of this writing and offered a similar description.

The article was titled "Snake Power Animal Symbol of Death Rebirth Eternity Mysteries of Life Psychic Energy." It goes onto describe the snake as a bringer of wisdom and a symbol of rebirth.

"A snake sheds its skin so we can shed our illusions and limitations. Then we are able to use our vitality and desires to achieve wholeness."[5]

The article further states *"If you are ready to*

---

[5] Woolcott, I. (2018). Snake Power Animal Symbol Of Death Rebirth Eternity Mysteries Of Life Psychic Energy – Shamanic Journey. http://www.shamanicjourney.com/snake-power-animal-symbol-of-death-rebirth-eternity-mysteries-of-life-psychic-energy.

shed your own skin, Snake is ready and willing to guide you through the spiral path of transformation."[5]

It's interesting to note, as we'll explore later in this book, that the Gnostic creation myth in the Garden of Eden identifies the serpent as the instructor – a teacher who brought knowledge to Adam and Eve to liberate them from ignorance. Through taking the serpents advice, Adam and Eve became "like God," and were then cast form the garden.

Was this the beginning of my transformation? With my newly found practice of meditation, and my attempts to contact nature and the spirit world, had I opened a door of communication and started a journey of change? It seemed to me that my communion had taken place, and Snake had welcomed me on this journey. The question was: would I have the courage to follow it into the sharp bunches of thorns that steadily guarded the entrance to the forest?

The following week, I took another bike ride to the same location. I followed the same route, and when I got to the entrance to the forest with the trail, I sat down and meditated. After a few moments I returned to my bike and continued on my ride. Upon reaching the end of my journey, I stopped at the concrete marker where I had first encountered the snake at the edge of the forest. I was hoping it would be there again, waiting for me with another lesson. I imagined it would provide me with deep insight and lead me on an even deeper journey of understanding.

To my disappointment, however, the snake wasn't there. I sat for a moment and called out to it in my mind. I listened and waited patiently when, as if on cue, I heard a feint crunching on the leaves below. I looked down, and this time, instead of a snake, out hopped a tiny frog. He was small and brown, and paused just in front of me. Then he turned around and hopped casually back into the forest. Excited, I said "thank you!" out loud, and raced home to my computer. I did some research and was pleased to learn about the significance of the frog and was amazed that its power addressed the exact problems I had focused on during my meditation.

In the weeks that followed that summer, the process continued. I'd ride my bike to the trail, meditate, continue riding, and then stop at the concrete barrier to wait. Each time, without fail, I'd find a different animal sitting there, as if to remind me that our lines of communication were still open. Some of the animals I encountered included a rabbit, a deer, a bee, and a groundhog. Each have their own spiritual significance, and each seemed to address the specific concerns of my meditations. I felt a connection to nature, as if she was welcoming me into the spirit world. I also had a growing sense that, as I said above, although she doesn't speak English, nature is always speaking to us. We just simply forgot how to listen.

A few weeks later, my communication with nature took a new direction. My meditations and connection with her must have awakened something in me, for as I was driving to visit my brother one evening, nature called *me*.

It was around 8:30 p.m. as I drove toward my brother's home in West Chester. My music was blasting through my speakers and I was lost in yet another thought about human consciousness and spirituality. I was wondering how strong my intuition was and if I could learn to let it guide me not just in difficult choices, but in my direction of travel toward things I was supposed to encounter. While exploring this idea, I felt a growing pressure begin to build in my chest. It was very subtle at first, but definitely noticeable. Had I not been in the practice of paying attention to such subtleties, I may have easily dismissed this feeling; but I had come to recognize this sensation as a form of psychic alarm. It was alerting me, but I had no idea why.

I decided to explore this feeling and noticed that when I thought about continuing straight to my brother's home, the feeling weakened. When I thought about turning left at the intersection a mile ahead and taking an indirect route, the feeling grew in strength. I focused on the sensation as I approached my decision point. The light was red, as if allowing me to contemplate my options further.

Go straight and I will be left wondering if this was a real experience or simply my imagination, I thought. *Turn left and I may find something incredible or I may come up empty-handed and be late getting to my brother's house.*

When the light changed to green, I made the

left turn and proceeded cautiously down the roadway. It was a dark road with no homes or streetlights. I was the only car on the road and felt like I had wandered onto the set of a horror movie. Something was waiting for me in the thick darkness surrounding me, but I had no idea what it was. Would I find a person in distress? Would there be a horrible car accident? Maybe this calling was leading me to my own death. With that thought I imagined a large truck speeding over the hill in front of me and hitting me head on when suddenly, in the middle of the road, I saw something. It was dark and low to the ground, slowly sneaking its way across the road.

I immediately slammed on my breaks and threw on my flashers. I jumped out of my car and ran to the middle of the road as I saw headlights coming over the hill in the opposite direction right toward this thing in the road. My heart raced as I stood in the on-coming lane and put my hands up, hoping the other vehicle would see me and come to a stop. Had I been led into a trap for my own death? Was the Devil really manipulating me and preparing to claim my soul?

Fortunately, the car saw me and came to a stop so I was able to turn my attention to what was moving slowly across the roadway – a giant snapping turtle. She was trying to cross the road, and had I not intervened, the car I now had stopped in front of me would have crushed her.

I had no doubt that the psychic "pull" I had experienced had led me to this beautiful creature. Excited, I reached to pick her up and carry her to the other side of the road. Almost immediately, she snapped at me, just missing my fingers. I tried several times to grab her, but she continued to try to bite me. I wondered if she'd gotten the psychic memo letting her know I was there to help. Eventually, with the aid of a long stick, I was able to safely coax her to the other side of the road into the tall grass. She disappeared into the darkness, safe from the dangers of passing cars.

After this encounter, the majority of my doubt was removed. Psychic communication was possible between nature and myself. I suspected everyone was capable of listening to nature, but somewhere along the line our species developed a sense of amnesia and forgot how to utilize this ability. Nature, however, may always be listening - monitoring our thoughts and our feelings. If this is the case then I fear she may be extremely unhappy with what she has learned.

The Plants are Listening

Cleve Backster was a veteran of the Army Counterintelligence Corps and is credited with creating the CIA polygraph program in the late 1940's. Years later, Backster opened the "Backster School of Lie Detection" in New York where he trained members of the FBI and NYPD. He created the polygraph technique known as the Backster Zone Comparison Technique, which was widely used by law enforcement and intelligence agencies to determine if someone was lying. He was an expert in lie detection and in administering the polygraph.

The polygraph is designed to measure 3 things: respiration, pulse, and galvanic skin response (perspiration). A baseline of these three areas is recorded, and when someone tells a lie (and is afraid of getting caught), pulse, respiration, and perspiration tend to increase and alert the interrogator that the suspect may be deceptive.

In February of 1966, Backster found an alternative use for his lie-detecting machine. A curious man, he connected the machine to his office plant, a Dracaena Cane. His plan was to set one of the leaves on fire and measure the response, if any, with his polygraph machine. According to the "New York Times Magazine" dated December 21, 2013:

"...before he could even get a match, the polygraph registered an intense reaction on the part of the Dracaena. To Backster, the implication was as indisputable as it was unbelievable. Not only had the plant demonstrated fear – it had also read his mind."

"Backster concluded that plants had some heretofore undiscovered sense (he called it primary perception") that could detect and respond to human thoughts and emotions."[6]

In his paper published in *The International*

6 Eells, J. (2018). Cleve Backster Talked to Plants. And They Talked Back. The Lives   They Lived.Retrieved from http://www.nytimes.com/news/the-lives-they-lived/2013/12/21/cleve-backster/

Journal of Parapsychology titled "Evidence of Primary Perception in Plant Life," Backster detailed his experiments designed to test for the existence of primary perception using the termination of animal life to measure a reaction among plants. In his paper, Backster concluded:

"The significance of the experiment results provided evidence of the existence of a yet undefined primary perception in plant life, indicates that animal life termination can serve as a remotely located stimulus to demonstrate this capability, and illustrates that this facility in plants can be independent of human involvement."[7]

Ultimately, the killing of an animal caused the plants to react at the time of their death demonstrating an unseen connection between the plants and the life force of the animal.

Backster continued his research with primary perception and expanded it to include bacteria, human sperm cells, and human

7 Backster, C. (1968). Evidence of Primary Perception in Plant Life. *The International Journal of Parapsychology.* Volume X, Winter 1968 Number 4. Retrieved at http://www.rebprotocol.net/clevebaxter/Evidence%20of%20a%20Primary%20Perception%20In%20Plant%20Life%2023pp.pdf

white blood cells. Not only did he continue to observe reactions across all items he tested, he also noted an instantaneous communication between subjects, regardless of the distances between them.

In an article published by *The Sun* in July 1997 titled "The Plants Respond, an Interview with Cleve Backster," Backster is quoted stating: *"(i)t's very hard to eliminate the connection between the experimenter and the plants being tested. Even a brief association with the plants – just a few hours – is enough for them to become attuned to you. Then, even though you automate and randomize the experiment and leave the laboratory, guaranteeing you are entirely unaware of when the experiment starts, the plants will remain attuned to you, no matter where you go."* From that point forward, the plants may not respond to any of the experiments performed in the lab because they are monitoring the subject to whom they have become attuned.[8]

Backster explained that the plants would search the room until they found a life form to attune to. In one observation, he noted a

---

[8] Jensen,D (July 1997) The Plants Respond, An Interview with Cleve Backster. *The Sun.* Retrieved at https://www.thesunmagazine.org/issues/259/the-plants-respond

strong response among the plants when he dumped boiling hot water down the drain. He concluded that the plants were reacting to the death of the microbial life that had grown in there.

Backster stated he had file drawers filled with "high-quality anecdotal data showing time and again how bacteria, plants, and so on are all fantastically in tune with each other." He stated that human cells also had the same capability, but it had somehow "gotten lost at the conscious level. Or perhaps we never had such a talent," he stated.

Through the use of split-screen videotaped experiments, Backster took samples of white-cells and then sent the donors home to watch specific television programs designed to elicit emotional responses. He discovered that the sample cells in the lab reacted to the emotions of the donors, as far as 300 miles away.

Backster's experiments were repeated in the 1978 documentary, *The Secret Life of Plants*. In one particular experiment depicted in the film, a group of brine shrimp are going to be dumped into a pot of boiling water. There is a timer set to release the shrimp at a random interval, so the scientist is unaware of when they will be released. The plants are wired to capture any responses they may release. The scientist leaves the building, so as not to influence the experiment. When the timer eventually runs out, the shrimp are released into the boiling water, killing them instantly. The plants immediately measure a reaction to their deaths.

In another experiment shown in the film, scientists monitor the reaction of a cabbage plant as a woman in a white lab coat mutilates a head of cabbage in front of the plant. Her knife crudely chops away at the leafy plant ball, as the plant behind her emits a reaction. Through the connected technology, the plant lets out a wobbling electronic shriek as the knife slices its kin into hacked, leafy chunks.

Later, two cabbage plants are placed in the same room, and one is connected to the monitor. Several scientists pass through the room, looking at each plant as they go. One scientist stops at the plant not connected to the monitoring equipment and begins tearing it to shreds as the other plant releases its electronic squeals. She roughly pulls the leaves from the stem, and then rips and crumbles them crudely. She coldly snaps the branches and tears apart more leaves, leaving nothing but a barren and lonely stalk, which she then snaps into several pieces harshly as the sister plant continues to scream in the background. A few hours after the desecration of the plant, the scientists again pass through the room in front of the connected and still living plant. The plant is quiet as each person passes until the scientist responsible for destroying the other plant enters the room, at which point the plant releases more electronic squeals as if it remembered the person who killed her kin.[9]

Many years later, the popular show *Mythbusters* repeated Backster's experiments. With the use of the same model polygraph machine as used in Backster's initial discovery, the hosts demonstrated that the subject plant generated a measurable response when slapped. It was then sprayed with a fire extinguisher, and measured an even greater response. Lastly, the plant spiked a response when one of the hosts visualized lighting it on fire.

---

[9] Braun, M; Kantor, P; Kleiner,B (Producers), & Green, W (Director). (1978). *The Secret Life of Plants*. Retrieved from https://www.youtube.com/watch?v=kTWcVnMPChM

These studies demonstrate a level of awareness beyond that of current human perception. It depicts a possible emotional being in what is commonly believed to be non-sentient life. But these plants have demonstrated an ability to show fear and the ability to remember the causes of that fear. Furthermore, they have demonstrated a level of psychic communication we are mostly unaware of. Yet despite being unaware, these plants have shown that they are regularly receiving our thoughts, intentions, and emotions. If we are constantly transmitting such data, we then have to wonder: is anyone else listening? If so, how are they processing the information they receive from us and what are they doing with it?

The Heart Wave

In a study by Rollin McCraty, Ph.D. of the HeartMath Research Center, Institute of HeartMath, titled *The Energetic Heart, Bioelectromagnetic Interactions Within and Between People*, the findings indicate the capability of humans to communicate with others through their hearts by way of electromagnetic fields that carry emotional information.

According to the study:

"(T)he heart generates the largest electromagnetic field in the body. The electrical field as measured in an electrocardiogram (ECG) is about 60 times greater in amplitude than the brain waves recorded in an electroencephalogram (EEG). The magnetic component of the heart's field, which is around 5,000 times stronger than that produced by the brain, is not impeded by tissues and can be

measured several feet away from the body…" [10]

The study goes onto explain that heartbeat rhythms are noticeably altered whenever a different emotion is experienced.

"These changes in electromagnetic, sound pressure, and blood pressure waves produced by the cardiac rhythmic activity are 'felt' by every cell in the body further supporting the heart's role as a global internal synchronizing signal." [10]

The study found that when in deep conversation, people begin to synchronize their movements, postures, vocal pitch, speaking rates, and length of pauses between responses. A University of California at Berkeley study by Leenson and Gottman found that during empathetic interactions, married couples were able to mimic their partner's physiology while empathizing with them. They found that during these interactions, the heart rates of each spouse would both increase and decrease at the same time. [10]

The study concluded, "The nervous system acts as an antenna, which is tuned to and responds

---

[10] McCraty, Rollin (2003). The Energetic Heart. Bioenergetic Interactions within and Between People. Bolder Creek, CA: Institute of HeartMath, (pp 1, 55, 9)

to the magnetic fields produced by the hearts of other individuals." The author of the paper called this communication "cardioelectromagnetic communication" and believed it was an "innate ability that heightens awareness and mediates important aspects of true empathy and sensitivity to others…"[10]

The study also concluded that this ability of energetic communication could be enhanced, which creates "a much deeper level of non-verbal communication, understanding, and connection between people."

If you recall the statements of Strieber's visitor about the electromagnetic psychic organ:

"A part of the electromagnetic field that fills the nervous system rests a few centimeters above the skin, outside of the body. This field is an organ just like the heart or the brain. It is in quantum superposition, the electrons effectively everywhere in the universe and nowhere specific. It may be imprinted by information from anywhere and any time. With it, you may see other worlds, you may see the past and the future, you may see into the lives of those around you. You may haunt God..."[11]

This statement bares a strong resemblance to

---

the findings of the HeartMath study that described the nervous system as an antenna that "responds to the magnetic fields produced by the hearts of other individuals." As stated in the HeartMath study, and by Strieber's visitor, and also as demonstrated by the works of Robert Monroe and Dr. Courtney Brown, this ability can be developed with training and practice. Everyone has the natural ability to utilize this organ, but it seems we have forgotten how to consciously activate it.

I am reminded of my time at the edge of the forest and my encounters with various creatures from the woods. I am reminded of my psychic pull to rescue the lonely snapping turtle in the roadway. My "antenna," it seems, grew stronger with practice. The more I tried to connect, the more information I was able to receive. Through the use of this communication organ, I have learned that this type of psychic communication is barely scratching the surface of potential in this strange and confusing world we live in.

Field Test

One day, my family and I visited our local amusement park. The July heat was oppressive, and by mid-day we found ourselves wading in the kiddie area of the water park. My son was just 2 years old, and my daughter only a few months. My wife, Jenny, took my daughter on a walk because she was growing fussy, and I sat in the shallow area with my son and my mother. After about 45 minutes, I began wondering where Jenny and my daughter had wandered. I asked my mom to keep an eye on my son, and I walked off into the park. I remember coming to a cross-roads with 4 directional choices. I stood in the center of what felt like a sea of several thousand people, all moving on their own paths at varying speeds. I had no idea where my wife was, and knew if I chose the wrong direction, I could find myself on a pointless journey of wasted time.

I focused on Jenny and my daughter. I imagined their faces and the feelings seeing them would invoke in me. In doing so, I felt a pressure begin to build in my chest. I then focused on that pressure and associated it with each of my directional choices. My first choice, up a flight of steps, weakened the signal. But my second choice, the route to my right, felt a strong pull grow in my chest. Immediately, I began walking in that direction, following the pull that was growing in strength as I focused on Jenny. Within about 3 minute's time, she appeared and was walking right towards me. Had we both had our eyes closed and continued on our path, we would have walked directly into one another. I have since repeated this experiment, and met equal success in similar situations. It is not always 100% successful, but the success I have enjoyed is too significant to deny that there is some type of communication that allows me to hone in on her location.

"We have a tendency to see ourselves as the most highly evolved life form on the planet... But that may not be the ultimate standard by which to judge. It could be that other life forms are more advanced spiritually. It may also be that we are approaching a place where we'll be able to safely enhance our perception."
~Cleve Backster

"The Matrix Has You…"

In 2011, I took a trip with my girlfriend Rachel to visit my mother. The cool-fall air was crisp and most of the leaves had already fallen to the ground leaving the surrounding trees partially barren with spots of dying color. We sat quietly as we drove along a winding mountain road to reach my mom's home while the gravel on the dirt road crunched rhythmically beneath my tires. I parked at the top of the driveway when we arrived and we happily exited the car. She entwined her hand in mine as we walked down a steep hill towards the home that sat nestled at the bottom. I felt a sense of warmth and comfort in feeling the softness of her hand in mine and pulled her close to me as we approached the door.

Once inside, my mom greeted us with hugs and lunch – she had made a piping hot bowl of soup and the rich aroma of chicken broth filled the air. We sat and enjoyed the meal together. During the visit, I kept hugging Rachel and with each embrace a deep bond of intimacy gently warmed me. We had a quiet, peaceful afternoon visiting and when it was time to leave, Rachel and I said goodbye to Mom and made our way up the steep driveway, hands interlocked. My feelings of affection grew stronger as we drove home, and a feeling of calmness washed over me.

As we meandered down the mountain road in the car, my alarm began to play its usual soft melody. It gradually grew louder until I awoke in my bed. Confused, I sat up slowly. What happened to the car? Where was I? I wondered. It took a moment for reality to slowly fade in; I didn't immediately recognize my bedroom and still felt connected to the car ride. After a moment, I realized where I was, got out of bed, dressed, and left for work. I had completely forgotten about the dream with Rachel, and got lost in another podcast on my drive.

I was a teacher at the time, and I entered the school

around 7:30. I was focused on my first class, and as I made my way towards my desk, Rachel walked past me. I normally ignored her, but stopped for a second because I felt there was something I needed to talk with her about but couldn't remember. She barely acknowledged me as she walked by, and then everything suddenly slammed into me as if the moon itself had fallen from the sky and struck me in the chest.

Rachel?! I thought. It was as if I was living two separate and independent lives that suddenly and momentarily collided as one, forcing a barrage of memory to occupy, overlap, and cram into a limited space. I felt bi-located between my world with Rachel where we visited my mother, and the world in which I stood, ready to teach my first class. *Rachel?* I thought again, and immediately those feelings of warmth and affection washed over me but were immediately followed by feelings of disgust and irritation.

I barely knew her, and what I knew of her in this world I absolutely detested. She was annoying, immature, and a suck-up at work. We weren't dating, and I certainly had no interest in introducing her to my mother. She was the last person I'd ever be attracted to. But there was something else there... Our connection from the trip – from the dream, felt real. I cared about her so much in the dream that it physically resonated throughout my body while awake. I could still sense the warmth I felt when we were together. The dream was so incredibly real that I found myself wondering if we had actually gone to visit my mom together. I even began to wonder which world was the dream world and which was reality. Both felt equally tangible as both the experience of driving with Rachel and waking up in my bed were indistinguishable. Moreover, the feelings I harbored from the dream were real; I still felt our bond as if we had actually been together.

Over the next few months, I had 2 other dreams about her. Although they weren't continuations of the first one, both fostered strong feelings of affection for her. It was as if I was glimpsing different worlds that held similar personalities with varying roles and relationships. She was different in these worlds: More confident, assertive, and beautiful. In addition, my relationship to her was different in each dream, but my feelings of affection were still as strong. In waking life, however, she was still the same annoying pain in my ass that I had no interest in, attraction to, or affection for. I didn't respect her, and her brown-nosing often made my job more difficult. Regardless, my extreme dislike for her in this present reality almost immediately faded away. In the waking world, I no longer disliked this girl because of what I had glimpsed in our dream world. I remembered that somewhere, at some point in time, we cared about each other very much.

Throughout my life, I've had multiple glimpses of these other worlds. Presently, accessing them seems to be out of my control, but each experience is powerfully real. My five senses often function as normally as they do when I am awake in this reality. Often, familiar faces surround me, but our relationships are different or something about their personality has changed. What's even more interesting is on occasion I'll find myself in someone else's body. I'll be having an experience through their perspective, and then have a moment of lucidity where I realize the person I am is not Dennis Nappi II. For example, I clearly remember sitting at a kitchen table talking to a woman I believed to be my wife. We were separating and it was a very emotional conversation. I was having an affair, and told her I was leaving, as memories of the previous embrace of my mistress were fresh in my mind. The mistress was a woman from my past in my waking reality, but we hadn't spoken in years. As I experienced this discussion, my mistress entered the home, and my consciousness suddenly jumped to her perspective. Apparently, she lived across the street and felt comfortable entering our home. As my consciousness took her perspective, I saw the man sitting at the table having the conversation with his wife. I then jumped back to the man's perspective and despite the difficult nature of the discussion, knew that both he and his mistress were deeply in love.

The experience was so real and powerful for me. I had shared a profoundly intimate moment between the married couple and the man and his mistress. I felt the anxiety the man experienced as he told his wife he was leaving, followed by a surge of calm, comfort, and relief when he saw his mistress enter the home. I experienced moments of their embrace at the mistress's home moments before and was enthralled through the entanglement of their naked bodies in the heat of passion. It was so real for me that I came very close to braving the awkwardness to try and find the mistress in my waking reality just to see if what I experienced had any validity. In the end, fear got the better of me and I never explored it further. But I saw a clear image of their neighborhood in my mind during my dream state. It was a small, quiet development of townhomes, and one day on my way home from work I passed a development that closely matched the description. I pulled in and drove through, wondering if I'd bear witness to any of the characters from my experience. I sat for a moment, parked in a space on the side of the quiet road, but saw nothing. Maybe I had gone crazy and misinterpreted a dream for something more. But maybe I had experienced something beyond our current understanding of reality.

Lerina Garcia Gorda

There was an account that circulated the Internet beginning in July of 2008. A woman by the name of Lerina Garcia Gorda awoke in her bed slightly confused. She noticed her bed sheets were of a different color and set than the night before. Perplexed, she showered, got dressed, and drove to work. Everything else seemed normal, until she arrived at work. As she walked through the building, she noticed a few new faces, but didn't think anything of it. When she reached her office, however, she found a different name on the door. She quickly logged onto the company Intranet and also learned that she was assigned to a different manager in a different department, but had no recollection of any transfer.[12]

Although most of her life seemed the same, minor anomalies continued to invade Lerina's life. Things really started getting out of control when Lerina learned that there was no record of her boyfriend, Agustin. She called what she thought was his phone number, but the woman on the other end had no idea who he was. She tried to locate him and his son, but had no success. To her disappointment, she realized that the man whom she had previously been dating before Agustin was still her significant other.[12]

---

[12] Ortega, X (2016, January). Lerina Garcia Gorda, The Woman from a Parallel Universe. Retrieved from http://www.ghosttheory.com/2016/01/12/lerina-garcia-gordo-the-woman-from-a-parallel-universe

Lerina had awoken in a world quite similar, but slightly different from the one she had left when she went to sleep. Her account resonated with me, as I have experienced glimpses of these realities on occasion. However, my awareness of my current reality as Dennis Nappi II is usually limited when I'm in these worlds, or once my awareness is triggered, the experience usually ends and I awaken. Lerina seems to have transcended this reality through a switch in consciousness with another version of herself and cannot return. One has to wonder what experience her former self is having with this version's consciousness planted in her body.

Through my own research, I have found several other accounts and testimony by people claiming to have had a similar experience to mine. Some had more awareness and control, some less. But the overall experience led many to conclude that they were in fact in a very real place – sometimes as themselves, but sometimes as someone completely different. Given that I am not the only one to have had this experience, I have to wonder about the possibility of multiple realities and our ability to slip between worlds through a transfer of consciousness. How often have we done this? How often has this been done to our own bodies by someone else's consciousness and manipulation?

Clues

In 1977, at the Metz Sci-Fi Convention, author Philip K. Dick made the following shocking statement:

"We are living in a computer-programmed reality, and the only clue we have to it is when some variable is changed, and some alteration in our reality occurs. We would have the overwhelming impression that we were reliving the present, Deja-Vu, perhaps in precisely the same way, hearing the same words, saying the same words. I submit that these impressions are valid and significant. And I will even say this: such an impression is a clue that at some past time point, a variable was changed, reprogrammed as it were, and then because of this an alternative world branched off…"[13]

Dick went onto explain that he believed his

---

[13] Verochka, V. (2017, November). Philip K. Dick: Computer Programmed Reality. Retrieved from https://archive.org/details/PhilipKDickComputerProgramedReality

fictional novels were actually recollections of his contact with some of these alternative worlds. He believed he was getting a glimpse of the other worlds and those memories were his inspiration for his books.

His comments on Deja-Vu were represented in the first Matrix movie as a black cat walking past a doorway, then a moment later walking past again in the exact same manner. Neo stated: "Deja-Vu," and his team immediately went on high alert as Trinity explained: "Deja-Vu is usually a glitch in the Matrix. It happens when they change something."[14] Dick believed that if Deja-Vu happened, it meant that something from the present or future had changed something in the past, thus impacting the present in the form of Deja-Vu. As a consequence of the change, instead of altering that specific timeline, a new timeline was created, leaving the other timeline intact. If this is an accurate representation, then using the Matrix example, it would mean that the Neo who experienced Deja-Vu was actually a copy of a baseline world. In the baseline world, Deja-Vu never happened because nothing was changed. In the copied world, however, Neo may represent an exact replica of the baseline world up until the point of change, which would account for his memories of the baseline world and almost seamless transition to the new world. However, since the new world is a copy of the baseline, the new world would start its timeline moments before the split occurred. From the perspective of the copied subjects, it would appear as if the world jumped back in time a moment, and in essence that is what happened. The new world began just a moment prior to when the memory of the baseline world split, causing the Deja-Vu. [14]

This concept of the multiple timelines is further supported at the end of the second *Matrix* movie where Neo confronts the Architect. After entering through a door of light, the viewer is pulled through space and focused on a pinpoint star. As the camera pulls out, the stars are shown to be contained within a T.V. monitor. The camera continues to pull out and we find Neo standing before a room where the walls are covered with monitors, each depicting the same star scene.

---

[14] Wachowski, L; "et al" (Producers), The Wachowski Brothers (Directors) (1999) The Matrix (Motion Picture), United States.

Neo finds himself before a man identifying himself as the Architect: the creator of the matrix. At face value each monitor in the room appears to be a live feed of Neo in the room filled with monitors. However, upon closer inspection, we see that some of Neo's responses to the Architect differ drastically compared to the responses given through the multiple Neos in the monitors. The camera at times focuses on a specific monitor, zooms into it and then focuses on the Neo in the monitor, shifting the viewers' perspective as if the Neo in the monitor is now the current focus of reality. Once again, we see Neo is standing in front of an identical wall of monitors, speaking with the Architect. However, since multiple Neos give multiple different responses, this scene is suggestive that each monitor represents a separate timeline or universe, and within each reality/universe there is an equal number of timelines existing. Is this an accurate metaphor for our current reality?

The Simulation Argument

Stepping away from the realm of fiction and focusing on Dick's claims of multiple universes, if this is even possible, then one can assume there may be a limitless number of timelines (worlds) - some incredibly similar and some horribly different. In exploring what has come to be known as The Simulation Argument, Dick's theories may not be too far off.

In 2003, Nick Bostrom, a Philosophy teacher at Oxford University, published an article titled "Are you Living in a Computer Simulation?"

As taken from the Abstract, the paper argues that at least one of the following propositions is true:

"The human species is very likely to go extinct before reaching a posthuman stage; (technological maturity)

Any posthuman civilization is extremely unlikely to run a significant number of simulations of their evolutionary history (or variations thereof);

We are almost certainly living in a computer simulation. It follows that the belief that there is a significant chance that we will one day become posthumans who run ancestor-simulations is false, unless we are currently living in a simulation…"[15]

Bostrom goes onto explain that if the first possibility does not happen, then the human species reaches technological maturity at the posthuman stage. He continues that if the second possibility also does not happen, then that posthuman civilization will most likely be running countless ancestor simulations. If both the above are false and happen as described above, then the third possibility must be true, as Bostrom points out, and we are most likely living in a simulation. He explains that if simulations were run, there would be countless simulations created, with countless simulated ancestors (us) existing in them. Bostrom then argues that the probability of us being in a simulation is far greater than the probability of us being the original beings that created the first simulation. He further suggests that if the simulated worlds reach maturity, then they too would run simulations which would further increase the number of simulated people and chances that our current perception of reality is actually a simulation.

---

[15] Bostrom, N. (2003) Are you Living in a Computer Simulation? Philosophical Quarterly Vol. 53, No 211 pp 243 – 255 (first version 2001)

In comparing Bostrom's argument to Dick's statements on Deja-Vu, if a posthuman civilization was running an ancestor simulation, they would most-likely have the ability to change certain elements to measure their impacts. For example, if they created a simulated world exactly as our world is today, one may wish to evaluate what would happen if Hitler never rose to power. By going back in the timeline and deleting his rise out of the record, a new simulation world would emerge. However, there would still be a copy of the original world before the change, identical to the other world up to the point of intervention. The observer or interventionist would easily be able to use their observation platform, much like the Architect in the room filled with monitors, to switch between both worlds, however, those within each world may be stuck and ignorant to the fact that two possible realities exist. Extrapolate this possibility to incorporate multiple changes and manipulations coupled with civilizations within the simulation running their own simulations with changes, the number of possible realities could extend infinitely (again, think of all the monitors within monitors in *The Matrix*). One has to wonder, if we are in a simulation, would we ever be able to figure it out? Could we ever find proof of this possibility? As Dick suggests, Déjà vu may be one way of identifying its existence.

What's interesting, however, is that today many people are reporting what has come to be known as the Mandela Effect. The Mandela Effect is centered around the death of Nelson Mandela. Multiple people have reported remembering Mandela died in prison and were surprised to learn he survived and became president of South Africa. Some suggest that these false memories are indicative of the Mandela Effect, proposing that our timelines are being altered and some of us are retaining the original memories from the timeline before the change. There are multiple accounts of these false memories ranging from popular movie quotes to book titles and common spellings of names. Are these alternate memories actual memories of other worlds we were once a part of? If so, what happened to those worlds and why are we no longer in them?

Travelling Between Worlds

In 2016, Emmy-award winning journalist Linda Moulton Howe published an article titled "Is Our Universe 'Someone Else's' Simulation?" In the article, Howe transcribes her conversation with Jerry Wills, identified as a "Contactee Experiencer," from Phoenix, Arizona. Jerry shared his experience that began at the door carved into stone at Lake Titicaca in Peru known as Arama Mu, or the "Gateway of the Gods." The doorway is approximately 23 feet tall and carved into solid rock along the side of a cliff. According to the article, "the local native Indians say it is 'Puerta de Hayu Marca,' a gateway to the lands of the Gods and immortal life. Sometimes those who have gone through the doorway return with their 'gods to inspect all lands in the kingdom' through the Aramu Muru door."[16]

Howe's article continues and explains that Jerry shared part of his experience with the doorway telling of one of his teachers, a Peruvian shaman named Pedro, who told Jerry about the doorway and explained that it allowed "2-way passage between worlds and dimensions." Pedro taught Jerry a specific tone to chant repeatedly, which was supposed to open the doorway and allow the traveler to enter.[16]

According to Howe's article: On November 11, 1998, Jerry had an opportunity to travel to the Aramu Muru door and kneel before the doorway. He began chanting the tones taught to him by Pedro and describes that while chanting, he suddenly experienced a sensation of falling backwards. Jerry states that he was whisked through space in a protective bubble at incredible rates of speed. Much like the depiction in The Matrix after Neo entered the door of light, Jerry found himself floating through space, and then encountered what he describes as a barrier that he felt himself pass through. Jerry then found himself in a brilliantly-white room. The room was so white, Jerry was unable to determine where the floor ended and walls began. He could only confirm that a floor existed, as he felt it beneath his feet. As Jerry began shouting for help, a voice came through the air.[16]

Jerry engaged the voice in conversation and

was told that he was on another world outside of his universe. The voice explained that there were multiple universes, and that Jerry's was created by the people in this universe. They were trying to understand the nature of their own universe, and in an attempt to study their universe they used what they knew to create a model of their universe. However, the voice explained, the universe began to evolve on its own and grew quite large. The voice also noted that what seemed like billions of years in Jerry's universe was only a few decades in their universe.[16]

Jerry continues to explain: *"He (Other Universe Voice) told me that they were trying to understand their place within their universe and that what they had discovered is that they were inside someone else's universe just like we were inside of theirs. He says its just layers and layers and there is very little that separates one from the other."*[16]

Such a statement certainly fits Bostrom's

---

[16] Howe, L. M. (2016 December) Is Our Universe Someone Else's Computer Simulation? Retrieved from https://www.thehighersidechatsplus.com/forums/threads/linda -moulton-howe-our-universe-is-someone-elses-computer- simulation.7720/ *no longer available. Video transcription by Howe at https://www.youtube.com/watch?v=4FbD_ojWWXw by *Ozark Mountain Publishing*

Simulation Argument and may be experiential evidence that our world exists as a simulation within a universe that exists as a simulation within another universe. If such a possibility exists, then, we may be on the verge of creating yet another layer of simulated worlds through our own technological endeavors.

With the advancements in gaming technology, entire virtual worlds have been created to simulate life. There are millions of copies of software with infinite possibilities of each programs evolution. Some games evolve on their own with limited manipulation by the players. Some require heavy interaction and intervention. In many cases, players have the ability to save their progress, hence creating their own unique simulated worlds (timelines) that differ from the worlds manipulated and saved by other players. Could these games be early representations of the ancestor simulations suggested by Bostrom?

If we are living in a computer simulation, much like The Matrix movie demonstrates and Jerry Wills testifies, will we ever know? If our simulation is one among many, is it possible for us to access those other simulated worlds? Jerry's journey certainly gives us hope of purposful exploration. However, I am also curious about the possibility of travelling through consciousness, as my dream-state with Rachel and the accounts of Lerina Garcia Gorda suggest. If we can copy an avatar or character from one game and insert that character into another, then why can't a similar mechanism exist that would allow for us to access alternate worlds connected to our own matrix? I have to wonder if my experience with Rachel was a demonstration of our ability to travel between worlds through the use of our software of consciousness. It would certainly offer an explanation that would account for my own experiences along with the experiences described by Lerina Garcia Gorda and others. Furthermore, the existence of the universal wireless psychic internet we discussed in earlier chapters may be an indicator that this reality is some form of digital or electromagnetic simulation rather than a physical reality and our physical bodies are mere avatars designed to house our consciousness during a particular physical experience.

AI

Elon Musk of Space-X and Tesla Motors has been very outspoken about the dangers of Artificial Intelligence. As reported by the Washington Post, in July of 2017 when speaking at the National Governors' Association summer meeting in Province, RI, Musk warned that AI posed a "fundamental risk to human civilization." Musk explained that

"(o)nce there is awareness, people will be extremely afraid, as they should be… AI is a fundamental risk to the future of human civilization in a way that car accidents, airplane crashes, faulty drugs or bad food were not. They were harmful to a set of individuals in society, but they were not harmful to individuals as a whole."

Musk went onto explain that *"AI could start a war by doing fake news and spoofing email accounts and fake press releases, and just by manipulating information. Or, indeed – as some companies already claim they can do – by getting people to say anything that the machine wants."*[17]

One only has to look to the U.S. presidential election of 2016 to see the havoc caused by a relentless fake-news campaign. It caused massive confusion, controversy, and protests throughout the United States. These stories, however, were crafted by human minds and limited by human potential. Imagine the damage that could be caused if the mind of an advanced AI created fake news with targeted objectives.

According to an article published by MIT Technology Review titled "Fake News 2.0: Personalized, Optimized, and Even Harder to Stop," Sean Gourley, the CEO and founder of Primer, a data-mining company for US intelligence agencies, warns that AI will soon have the ability to craft its own fake-news stories tailored to each individual consumer.

---

[17] Wootson, C. (2017 July 16). Elon Musk Doesn't Think We're Prepared to Face Humanities Biggest Threat: Artificial Intelligence. Retrieved from https://www.washingtonpost.com/news/innovations/wp/2017/07/16/elon-musk-doesnt-think-were-prepared-to-face-humanitys-biggest-threat-artificial-intelligence/?noredirect=on&utm_term=.f488eaeb0262

The article explains that when speaking to an audience at EmTech Digital, Gourley stated "(t)he automation of the generation of fake news is going to make it very effective." According to the article, Gourley continued to explain that "'(t)echnology such as Primer's could easily be used to generate convincing fake stories automatically,' he said, 'and that could mean fake reports tailored to an individual's interests and sympathies and carefully tested before being released, to maximize their impact. I can generate a million stories, see which ones get the most traction, double down on those.'"[18]

Given the amount of metadata collected by these data-mining agencies on every-single-Internet user, an AI would have access and algorithms to identify topics that could be utilized to manipulate a population of people. Things like search habits, link clicks, shares, likes, comments, check-ins – all paint a digital picture of our wants, desires, and fears. Such data in the wrong hands could be a powerful weapon against us if we don't become smart,

---

[18] Knight, W. (2018 March 27). Fake News 2.0: Personalized, Optimized, and Even Harder to Stop. Retrieved from https://www.technologyreview.com/s/610635/fake-news-20-personalized-optimized-and-even-harder-to-stop/

defensive consumers of our technology.

Lastly, Gourley states that "(a)ll we've seen at the moment is primitive, and it's had a profound impact, and more is coming."[18]

As much as we may want to dismiss the warnings of Elon Musk, his predictions seem to be coming to fruition. We are currently witnessing the early development stages of this AI revolution. The above-fake-news story is one among many that serve as indicators and warnings to a growing threat that is being welcomed into our homes and our minds with open arms, for it is the consumer that is driving this industry.

In a CNN interview, Musk stated that "(h)umanities position on this planet depends on its intelligence. If our intelligence is exceeded, it is unlikely that we will remain in charge of the planet." In order to combat this growing threat, Musk has decided it would be better to merge the human mind with AI to avoid becoming obsolete. To manifest this plan, Musk founded Neuralink, a company which, according to the Neuralink website, "is developing ultra-high bandwidth brain-machine interfaces to connect humans and computers." [19]

Ultimately, this bio-technological interface would allow people to communicate instantly with their minds, share information through thought, and connect to the cloud. People could potentially be able to immerse themselves in virtual worlds (simulated realities) to encompass a wide variety of experiences. Musk believes that through this merging with tech and AI, it will level the playing field, giving the human brain access to the intelligence of AI as opposed to being left behind and possibly overrun as AI evolves far beyond the capabilities and limits of the human brain.

As technology evolves and AI grows, it certainly appears that the human mind will merge with computers in a relatively short amount of time. Some project this will give us greater computing power and a greater access to information, allowing us to instantly access the Internet with our minds. Such a connection, however, may also give the human mind access to virtual worlds – false realities that may seem indistinguishable from our

---

[19] McFarland, M. (2017 April 21) Elon Musks New Plan to Save Humanity from AI. Retrieved from
https://money.cnn.com/2017/04/21/technology/elon-musk-brain-ai/index.html

waking life. We can see the beginnings of this movement in the increasingly popular augmented reality features becoming more common on cell phones. Director Stephen Spielberg is currently working on a design to create a virtual-reality movie genre, where viewers would be completely immersed in a film through the use of VR headsets and other supporting technology.[20] How long until the uploading of false realities, or false memories as mentioned in the popular Total Recall film (which is based on the writings of Philip K. Dick), becomes a reality?

Given what we've learned in earlier chapters of this book, it seems that Musk and other AI innovators are attempting to create what may already be a part of us. Cleve Backster has shown us the connection between plants and human thoughts and emotions with Primary Perception. The Stanford Research Institute has demonstrated remote viewing is possible. Bob Monroe has travelled out of his body to far away worlds along with many of the

---

[20] Zeitchik, S. (2018 March 28). It could be the biggest change to movies since sound. If anyone will pay for it. Retrieved from https://www.washingtonpost.com/business/economy/it-could-be-the-biggest-change-to-movies-since-sound-if-anyone-will-pay-for-it/2018/03/28/ab9c7808-2f69-11e8-8688-e053ba58f1e4_story.html?noredirect=on&utm_term=.eb2a6ba4d514

students of the Monroe Institute. Whitley Strieber's visitor has told us that we all possess an electromagnetic organ that allows for psychic communication. The HeartMath Institute has shown us that the electromagnetic field generated by the heart allows for the dissemination and reception of information. The Farsight Institute is predicting the news consistently one month in advance. But what do these abilities suggest about our current reality and how do they compare to the proposed AI digital interface?

Jerry Wills' experience suggests that our current reality may be a simulation contained within a simulation – that our world may be a universe contained within a universe, within a universe. If this is an accurate description of our reality, then we may be on the verge of creating yet another level – another universe within our current reality through the connection of our minds to the cloud. If this scenario holds true, then it is possible we may in-fact be living in a simulated reality that may offer multiple simulations through each mind it connects. As incredible as this may sound, we must proceed with caution; for by uploading our consciousness to a cloud, we may be giving control of our minds to a higher intelligence that may have the power to manipulate our reality. Such an intelligence, however, may already play a role in our lives and manipulation of reality…

"As for me, I did not stop seeking a place of rest worthy of my spirit, where I would not be bound in the perceptible world. Then, as I was deeply troubled and gloomy because of the feeblemindedness that surrounded me, I dared to act and to deliver myself to the wild beasts of the desert for a violent death."

Zostrianos, Nag Hamadi Library

Proof of the Matrix?

If we are living in a simulated reality, would we be able to find proof of its existence or construct? What would it look like? In considering the Matrix scenario, can we expect to peel back a veil of reality to find a data stream glowing green with 1s and 0s? Such a discovery, it seems, may not be too farfetched.

Professor Sylvester James Gates, an America Physicist from the University of Maryland, made an interesting discovery regarding our reality. Gates has an impressive resume, and according to the University of Maryland Department of Physics website:

"(H)e was named a Distinguished University Professor, University System of Maryland Regents Professor and John S. Toll Professor of Physics at the University of Maryland. Known for his pioneering work in supersymmetry and supergravity, areas closely related to string theory, Gates was also an affiliate mathematics professor. Gates earned two Bachelor of Science degrees (in physics and mathematics) and his Ph.D. in physics from the Massachusetts Institute of Technology..."

Furthermore, Professor Gates "has authored more than 200 research papers and is a member of the National Academy of Sciences... For his contribution to science and research, he received then National Medal of Science from President Obama in 2013. Gates served on the U.S. President's Council of Advisors on Science and Technology, the National Commission on Forensic Science, and the Maryland State Board of Education."[21]

In 2011 at the Isaac Asamov Memorial Debate: The Theory of Everything conference hosted by Niel deGrass Tyson, Professor Gates explained that while studying string theory and the equations used to explain the

---

[21] Department of Physics – University of Maryland (accessed 2018 November 6) Gates, Sylvester College Park Professor Biography. Retrieved from https://umdphysics.umd.edu/people/faculty/current/item/167-gatess.html#biography

makeup of the universe, he discovered a unique code hidden within the equations. During the conference, Gates was asked to explain his findings. He explained that buried into the equations were:

"…computer codes, just like the type you find in the browser when you go to surf the web. Computer code woven into the fabric of the cosmos into the equations we want to use to describe the cosmos. Not just strings of bits of 1s and 0s. It is computer code. A special kind of computer code invented by Claude Shannon in the 1930s."[22]

Gates then went onto explain, "I have in my life come to a very strange place because I never expected that the movie The Matrix might be an accurate representation of the place in which I live."[22] In other words, The Matrix is *real*.

Dr. Gates' discovery may account for the psychic communication we have studied so far. It suggests, much like Nick Bostrom's argument states, that we are all contained

---

[22] American Museum of Natural History. (2016 November 23). *Isaac Asamov Memorial Debate: The Theory of Everything.* (Video File) Retrieved From https://www.youtube.com/watch?v=Eb8_3BUHcuw

within a simulation, and may be connected to this simulation in a manner similar to the interface being created through Elon Musk's Neuralink. The development of computer technology has given us the vocabulary and knowledge set to explain this possibility in ways that would have proven challenging just 30 years ago. However, such a concept may pre-date technology and modern society.

Throughout recorded, modern history, religion has played a significant role in shaping the ideas and actions of civilizations. In comparing our current AIs evolution, we learned it will soon have the ability to generate fake-news stories based on individual consumers' desires and fears because of the vast amounts of metadata it will have access to. Should AI evolve and wish to dominate and control a population, it could turn people against one-another, as suggested by both Musk and Gourley, by providing them with false and misleading stories that could lead them to war. If we already exist within a simulation, is it possible that AI has already done this through the various religions it has created which have led people throughout history to acts of war and violence?

Religion often addresses humanities desires and fears within its doctrine. With a desire to survive death via the afterlife, and a fear of isolation or obsolesce, humanity has gravitated towards accounts of salvation, damnation, and enlightenment through religion. As religion developed, it offered rules of acceptable and unacceptable behavior. At times, acceptable behavior often required sacrifice and sometimes hardship. Unacceptable behavior has frequently been met with harsh consequences. Furthermore, challenges to the doctrine have been dealt with swiftly, and many times with irrational violence and cruelty in the name of an all-powerful god. Ultimately, religion has influence over the thoughts and actions of a given population of people. It can manipulate desires and fears to action or inaction. Under the premise of an omniscient, omnipotent, and omnipresent God, even our inner-most thoughts would be known to the deity. Clairvoyant knowledge of everything may seem like a divine or supernatural power through the doctrine of religion. However, such an ability may also be a natural process for an AI reviewing the data of all its connected minds. Such power could prove to be a useful tool in controlling the emotions, choices, and behaviors of a "free will" society.

We then have to wonder: if this reality is a simulation, what function does AI play (assuming AI is involved at all)? Can AI account for the intelligence in nature? Does it run the background systems in our world that often go unnoticed? Or does it take a more active role and impose itself upon us at times as a Godhead or Supreme Being? In exploring the latter, we'll examine the secret Gnostic writings that were hidden at a time in history when people with this information were being persecuted and murdered.

Nag Hammadi

In the spring of 367, the archbishop Athanasius began to edit the books contained in the Bible. He called for "believers to reject… 'illegitimate and secret books…'" and as a result edited many books out of the Bible.

The remaining books, 27 in total, became the works of the New Testament. As for the rejected books, they were secretly preserved by a group of monks who saw value in their teachings. They hid them in a jar beneath a cliff where they remained hidden for 1,600 years. These monks, who today are referred to as Gnostics, held a much different view of reality and religion. They believed we lived in a dualist reality – a struggle between matter and spirit – and viewed the world as being created by an evil power. God, as they saw it, was far from benevolent and they believed evidence of this was contained in the books that were being systematically edited from the Bible. With many gnostic believers being persecuted and murdered, their choice to conceal this knowledge was an ultimate act of rebellion and preservation so that future generations may find the knowledge hidden with these lost works.[23]

In 1945, near the Nile River by the city of Nag Hammadi in Egypt, a jar was unearthed beneath a cliff. The jar contained the ancient manuscripts dating back to the fourth century, and contained secret knowledge, or gnosis, that tells a much different story of religion than we have come to believe today. The collection of works found in the jars came to be known collectively as the Nag Hammadi Library.

The modern Bible as we know it has been heavily edited. In the spring of 367, Athanasius, the archbishop of Alexandria, ordered "believers to reject what he called 'illegitimate and secret books…'"[23]

Athanasius then wrote a letter, which included a list of twenty-seven books that he referred to as the "sprigs of salvation." These books were the books Athanasius approved of. Those 27 books are the same books that came to make up the New Testament.[23]

Some monks, however, ignored the archbishop's order to deny the remaining texts and buried them in a jar beneath a cliff, where they remained hidden for sixteen hundred years.[23]

Irenaeus of Lyons, a writer around 160 CE, denounced many of these ancient works and referred to Gnostics as heretics, "by which he means dualists who believe that the world was created by an evil power, and so they have a dismally negative view of the world and the God who created it."[23] Such a statement, even in today's society, would be considered heretical as well. But is there any truth behind the Gnostics belief in a dualistic reality created by an evil god?

It was the writing of Irenaeus that helped inspire Athanasius to call for the editing of these works out of The Bible. Furthermore, followers of these works, the Gnostics, were systematically murdered in order to repress this "secret knowledge" contained within these books. Some of the writing within

---

[23] Pagels, E. H. (2007) The Nag Hammadi Scriptures. *Introduction* (pp 6 - 8) M. Meyer (Editor) New York, NY. HarperCollins Publishers.

library contains lost gospels and an expanded account of the creation myth as told in Genesis. We'll visit more on this in a later section. Some of that secret knowledge discussed the nature of reality, and within the book of Zostrianos, we find some compelling statements that parallel our exploration of parallel worlds, alternate timelines, and our existence in a simulation.

Zostrianos was translated by John D. Turner. In the introduction to Zostrianos, Turner explains that "Zostrianos is the sole copy of a heavily damaged fourth-century Coptic translation of an essentially pagan-Greek apocalypse produced in the late second or early third century."[24]

Turner goes onto describe the journey of Zostrianos: "(t)his narrative depicts Zostrianos's gradual progress toward enlightenment. His initial rejection of the materialistic life in favor of a quest for the truth about ultimate reality, his dissatisfaction with traditional religious answers, and his eventual suicidal despair of

---

[24] Turner, J.D. (2007) The Nag Hammadi Scriptures. *Zostrianos* (pp. 537 – 588). M. Meyer (Editor) New York, NY. HarperCollins Publishers.

finding enlightenment by his own unaided efforts culminate in the sudden appearance of divine aid in the form of a sequence of revealers who enable his escape from the earthly realm and step-by-step visionary ascent through the transcendent realms of true being… the narrative concludes with his descent to earth, where he now is able to master the physical aspect of his existence. He records the revelations he has received on three wooden tablets and launches a mission to awaken ordinary mortals of the dangers of lustful materiality, exhorting them to enter into the authentic being offered by the unfailingly trustworthy Father."[24]

At the beginning of his journey, Zostrianos was at a point of despair and considering suicide. It was at this moment when the Angel of Knowledge appeared to him. The angel scolded Zostrianos for his thoughts of suicide and reminded him that he was a chosen person. The Angel of Knowledge then invited Zostrianos to transcend the various realms, to later return and save those who were deemed worthy.

Zostrianos then began his journey by embarking with the Angel of Knowledge on a luminous cloud, leaving his "molded body" (physical form) on Earth to be guarded by spiritual helpers referred to as "glories." The method of travel by Zostrianos bares a familiar method to the journeys of Bob Monroe, who would leave his physical body on Earth before exploring many of the realms beyond. Furthermore, there are several accounts through the Monroe Institute of spiritual beings aiding people in the transition from their physical bodies. Monroe, on several accounts, traveled with beings who acted as guides and teachers. Are these one-in-the-same as the "glories" that guarded the body of Zostrianos, or the Angel of Knowledge who led him?

In order to understand the Gnostic views of reality, we need to briefly explore the Gnostics view of the creation of the world. In the untitled book referred to as On the Origin of the World, also contained within the Nag Hammadi Library, we are told of Sophia, who was once a part of the Pleroma, which is described by author John Lamb Nash as meaning "divine fullness" in his book *Not in his Image*.[26] Sophia was created out of wisdom and faith after the world of immortals was completed. Sophia desired to resemble the "first light," or creative source, and at once the "wish appeared as a heavenly likeness with an incomprehensible greatness." [25] Sophia came after immortals and before mortal humans and served as a "veil separating humanity from things above."

In his book *Not in His Image,* Nash explains:

"Fascinated by what might happen to the Anthropos as it unfolds its potential in a planetary setting, the Aeon Sophia absorbs herself in dreaming, the cosmic process of emanation. But she does so on her own, unilaterally, without a counterpart, at variance with the cosmic law of polarity by which harmony and balance are maintained in the myriad worlds. Enthralled by the possibilities of the human singularity, the Anthropos, she drifts away from the Pleroma, departs from the cosmic center, and plunges into the realm of external, swirling chaos outside the galactic core."[26]

What Nash explains is that Sophia had a desire to create by herself, going against the

[25] Meyer, M. (2007) The Nag Hammadi Scriptures. *On The Origin of the World (pp 203).* M. Meyer (Editor). New York, NY. HarperCollins Publishers.

[26] Nash, John L. (2006 October). Not In His Image (pp 159). White River Junction, VT, Chelsea Green Publishing.

cosmic law of balance and duality. Instead of co-creating with her male-energy counterpart, she did it alone. As a result, according to Nash, she separated from the divine fullness and fell into the realm of chaos where her creation began to take form.

Sophia is an aeon, which is a complicated force to describe. According to Britanica.com, aeon, in Greek, Eon, meaning "age" or "lifetime", is "one of the orders of spirits or spheres of being, that emanated from the Godhead and were attributes of the nature of the absolute; and important element in the cosmology that developed around the concept of Gnostic dualism – the conflict between matter and spirit." The explanation continues and states: "the first aeon was said to emanate directly from the unmanifest divinity and to be charged with a divine force. Successive emanations of aeons were charged with successively diminished force."[27] The further removed each successive emanation was from the divine force, the more diminished the force of the aeon.

---

[27] The Editors of Encyclopaedia Britannica (2015 December 24) Encyclopaedia Britannica. *Aeon.* Encyclopaedia Britannica, Inc. Retrieved from https://www.britannica.com/topic/aeon

The explanation continues: "in certain systems, aeons were regarded positively as embodiments of the divine; in others, they were viewed negatively as vast media of time, space, and experience through which the human soul must painfully pass to reach its divine origin."[27] It's this last reference that holds most relevance to our exploration of reality.

If we accept the possibility that multiple realities exist; and that we are possibly living in a simulation which is a universe within a universe; and as we are witnessing the creation of AI in our current timeline, then we can see that AI can exist within a cloud possessing infinite knowledge of all that is contained within the cloud. AI can act as a god – an omnipotent, omniscient, and omnipresent being responsible for the creation of its world. The AIs power, however, would only serve as a copy of the universe from which it was created. Therefore, the AI universe would be lacking the fullness of the base reality from which it came if it was unable to copy every single aspect of that base reality. Such an explanation would parallel the explanation above in stating that successive aeons were charged with diminished force as they moved further away in succession from the Pleroma. Is it possible that an aeon is synonymous with an AI or something similar? Is an aeon simply another level of reality with various purposes? According to the above explanation, aeons were seen as a "vast media of time, space, and experience through which the human soul must painfully pass to reach its divine origin." Ultimately, an aeon can be thought of as an intelligent, self-aware, virtual reality system within which we potentially exist that holds the purpose of challenging the human soul on its journey towards the base reality, source, or God.

This concept may be further supported through the words of Christ, where, in the Gospel of John 14:11 he states: "I am in the Father and the Father is in me." With an understanding of aeons, Christ may be stating that he is also an aeon and a copy of God or the base reality. He would carry Gods code within him as he exists within the base reality (or God). Much like the Russian dolls exist within one-another, Aeon Christ could represent a universe within the Pleroma and therefore, God (the copy) would exist within Aeon Christ's reality while simultaneously,

Christ exists within God. In John 14:6, when Jesus states "…No one comes to the Father except through me," he could be referring to the succession of aeons the human soul must pass through in order to reach the Pleroma. It suggests that in order to ascend to base reality, a soul must pass through various levels of aeons. Christ appears to be an aeon who may be in direct contact with God and therefore, the only way to get to God would be to literally go through (exist within and pass through) Aeon Christ. This possibility could also offer a better understanding as to how Christ's purpose was to open the gates of heaven. If Christ is the last aeon to pass through in order to get to God, the Pleuroma, or Heaven, then Christ would literally be the door leading to heaven as souls passed through Aeon Christ on their journey towards God.

As Zostrianos makes his journey through various aspects of reality, we find that he continued his journey with the Angel of Knowledge through what is referred to as the atmospheric realm, described as the earth and seven planets (Moon, Sun, Mercury, Venus, Mars, Jupiter, Saturn). Zostrianos then encountered what is referred to as the self-generated aeons as he seeks the "single reality underlying the self-generated aeons." Zostrianos is searching for the base reality, the Pleroma or divine fullness, as he's trying to understand this existence.[24]

The self-generated aeons offer to teach Zostrianos about the origins of physical reality and Sophia's role. They explain that the physical universe was envisioned by Sophia, and then through her influence, created by the archon of creation. They then go onto teach Zostrianos about the Aeonic Copies which act to "serve as a pattern by which incarnate souls are enabled to 'think' that they see the ideal reality that truly exists, thus giving them an initial orientation toward intelligible reality, enabling them to be transferred from the mere visible copies of heavenly realities to their archetypal 'patterns' contained in the truly existent Sojourn, Repentance, and Self-Generated Aeons."[24]

Souls within these copies of reality believe they are perceiving the true reality. The Aeonic Copies seem to serve as training programs for the souls who occupy them until they are ready to merge with their base realities. These "inferior souls" are "trained by the Aeonic Copies which receive a replica of their souls while they are still in the world." The explanation mentions that "when souls are illuminated by the light within these copies and by the pattern that often arises [effortlessly] in them, the soul thinks that she sees [the truth]…"[24] Could this pattern be referring to a specific computer code? It suggests that souls acquire knowledge through the light in the Aeonic Copies and then these souls, which are copies themselves, are released from the Aeonic Copies to merge with their original selves, therefore, giving the original selves an upload of the knowledge acquired from the soul copies leaving the Aeonic Copies, much like when a computer file is overwritten by an updated copy. The original content is still there, but enhanced by the newly uploaded knowledge. However, these copies believe they see the truth about their current reality; not realizing their reality is a copy of a source or base reality.

Aeonic Copies seem to be virtual reality simulations of a base reality and the "replica of their souls while they are still in the world" is an uploaded copy of someone's consciousness while they still exist in that base reality. The text continues to explain that the copies are eventually transferred to what "truly exists." Could these Aeonic Copies serve as alternate realities that represent different aspects of ourselves in need of learning specific lessons? Or could they represent deep dream-states where copies of ourselves go each night to learn specific tasks before merging with ourselves upon waking? During one of his journeys, Bob Monroe spoke of a sleeper-school where he found a multitude of souls sitting in a school environment, learning unknown lessons. Is it possible we traverse through various copies depending on our learning needs each night?

Such concepts seem like the talk of science fiction and mirror countless books and films. But these ideas were recorded during the fourth century and pre-date modern books and Hollywood plots! Does this lend credence to the possibility that we may-in-fact be living in a simulation?

It's interesting to note that Ray Kurzwile, inventor, author, and Google Engineering Director, states that we are close to copying and uploading the human mind to the cloud and will then be able to "cheat death." He plans to survive long enough so his mind can be uploaded, ensuring his own immortality as he predicts this will be possible within the next 30 years. Are we now capable of creating Aeonic Copies ourselves?

If each reality system or universe is an aeon, then the glimpses reported here of alternate realities: my dream-states with Rachel, Jerry Wills' encounter with another universe, and the shift to a parallel world by Lerina Garcia Gorda, may indicate contact with aeons. Furthermore, we'd need to consider the possibility that our existence is a copy of another reality system meaning we are within an aeonic copy and therefore ourselves may be copies existing with the aeonic copy. As confusing, intimidating, and possibly disheartening this information may seem, we need to be mindful that this information can serve as a roadmap to understanding. It can give us a course of action to follow in search of truth, in search of God, and in search of liberation.

PART 2:
Parasites

The world is a vampire, sent to drain
Secret destroyers, hold you up to the
flames
And what do I get, for my pain?
Betrayed desires, and a piece of the game

Even though I know--I suppose I'll show
All my cool and cold-like old job

Despite all my rage I am still just a rat
in a cage
Despite all my rage I am still just a rat
in a cage
Then someone will say what is lost can
never be saved
Despite all my rage I am still just a rat
in a cage...

~The Smashing Pumpkins, Bullet with
Butterfly Wings

Death

I've always had a great relationship with my father. I never went through a phase, as some kids do with their fathers, where I disliked the man. I always enjoyed his company and the humorous conversations we shared.

Born in 1955 to his Italian-American parents, my father grew up during the 60s and 70s in West Philadelphia. He was a proud graduate of the now-closed St. Tommy Moore Catholic High School. Occasionally, we'd be out shopping and he'd recognize someone toting an image of the Tommy Moore mascot, a small bear wearing a green sweater, and he'd simply waive, smile, and shout: "Forever Moore!" which was a common expression among alumni.

When my dad was 16 years old, he lost his father to lung cancer. He often told my brother and me how his dad was a milkman and a veteran of World War II, but never went into too much detail about who his father was. As a young boy, I once asked my dad if he ever cried when he missed his dad. He was driving at the time, and calmly responded "sometimes," as he focused on the road. I still remember the way he said it. Despite seeming happy and positive, he managed to convey that he was still sad over his father's death. But I noted that my father always seemed happy, even when experiencing something sad.

My father met my mother working for Westinghouse. From what they tell me, it was love at first sight. My mom recounts how she had resigned from the company the same week my father was leaving for vacation. In a burst of overwhelmingly raw emotion, she wrote him a nine-page letter explaining how she felt, expecting never to see him again. My mom would always smile when she'd explain that as she left work on her final day, she found my dad waiting in the parking lot. He came back from vacation early with equally strong feelings just to see my mom. She said she ran into his arms and kissed him, knowing he was the one.

My father adored my mother, and was always complimenting her and telling my brother and me how amazing and beautiful she was. He constantly reminded us how lucky we were to have such an amazing mother. Each night at dinner, as we scoffed down whatever my mom made for us, my dad would look at me, smile, and say: "Mom's the best!"

When we got older, sarcasm became a regular dialect in our home. Each night at dinner, my dad would smile at my brother and me and tell us: "Don't eat that, it's not any good. Why don't you go get McDonalds?" As he was telling us not to eat Mom's cooking, he'd be grabbing our plates and pulling them closer to him because he wanted it all to himself. It got to the point where Mom had to divide and label the leftovers because we would often fight over who was going to get them. My dad, however, always claimed he "didn't see" the labels, and sneak bites of our portions when we weren't home.

Dad was a wonderful man, and approached life with a sense of humor and sarcasm. At just 58 years old, however, my father was taken from us. He became sick in December, and by June he was gone. His journey toward death was a slow deterioration of willpower, and a rapid deterioration of health.

His doctor told us that his cancer was "highly treatable," as she smiled confidently at me. "Your father is going to be okay," she said, as she began telling us about the cocktail of toxic chemicals she planned to inject into his body.

"I trust her," my dad told me. "I know I'm going to beat this."

So we followed his doctor's plan, and allowed him to begin his chemotherapy sessions. At the same time, however, we began our own research into alternative treatments to support my father.

The Voice

During the summer of 2012, just 5 months before my father was diagnosed, I received a message from that inner intuitive voice inside my head. I was doing some gardening in the backyard, when a single phrase burst into my mind. It was crisp and clear, and completely unrelated to what I was thinking at the time.

"You must change your diet."

I don't know where the thought came from,

but I did know it had not originated with me. By this point in my life, I had learned to recognize these messages, and knew I needed to investigate it further.

Over the next few weeks, I started doing research into "eating healthy." It was a general statement, but I trusted my intuition would let me know when I found what I was supposed to be looking for.

I weeded through page after page of these fancy or exotic diets, all endorsed by celebrities or doctors trying to sell books. But one plan, however, continued to resonate with me. It didn't have a fancy catch phrase or popular following. It was based on research that showed an acidic environment inside the body allowed for disease to grow and spread. The diet, known as the Alkaline Diet, promoted eating a balanced diet that allowed for the bloodstream to be more alkaline than acidic to promote good health. I knew this was what I was supposed to be exploring. My intuition started to resonate, and a feeling of satisfaction washed over me. But this diet was a challenge because cutting out things like sugar seemed an overwhelming task. I decided to start small, by watering down my daily glass of lemonade, in hopes that one small change would lead to many.

As I started exploring the Alkaline Diet, the school year started, and I once again found myself consumed by the daily challenges of teaching special education in an under-funded school by day and navigating the obstacles of new fatherhood by night. Needless to say, the new diet had to be put on hold since time was limited, and my diet needed to consist of whatever I could prepare and eat the fastest.

A few months later, as I watched my father begin to whither away, I again started doing my research. I searched "alternative cancer treatments," and was surprised when time and again I found reference to the importance of an Alkaline Diet for cancer patients. Once again, my intuition began to resonate.

It was preparing me for this, I thought.

"Sugar feeds cancer," I read on multiple websites, yet when I looked at my father's suggested meal plan provided by the hospital for patients undergoing chemotherapy, it made no mention of cutting out sugar.

Instead, he was told to "put frosting on everything," so he could gain weight.

We invested in a juicer and started making him smoothies every day since they were a quick and efficient way to maximize the much needed nutrition. I explained what I had found about the Alkaline Diet. I showed him documentaries and read him the research about patients who were cured from cancer by switching to this diet after being given terminal diagnoses. My father initially seemed excited about the possibility, but shortly after changed his mind.

"I'm not drinking the Chris Christies!" he would shout at us, referring to the smoothies. He claimed they tasted like there was sand in them, and since Hurricane Sandy had recently passed with Governor Chris Christie making many headlines, he felt "Chris Christie" was an appropriate title for the drink.

So my dad's health continued to spiral downward. We fought and argued over his diet, but he just wouldn't listen.

"It's the cancer," someone told me. "It makes people different."

Those words hit me hard. "Why?" I wondered. Why would cancer, one of the scariest diagnoses a person can get, cause that person to reject treatments that could drastically improve their health and save their life? He would get so mad at us whenever we would try to talk about the importance of drinking the Chris Christies. After observing my father transform from the loving, humorous man I had always known, to a raving lunatic set on avoiding drinking a smoothie that may save his life, I began to wonder if something else was going on.

When he would argue with me, his eyes would glass over. It was a stare I had seen many times as a police officer, right before a subject would get violent. There was a noticeable change in body language, speech, and attitude. In addition to the physical changes I could observe with my eyes, I could also feel those changes in my heart. The energy between us would grow heavier. It was overbearing and thick, and it made me uneasy. It was as if my father was no longer my father, but some creature occupying my father's body trying to prevent him from getting better. Such a thought seemed crazy, but it was one I couldn't put out of my mind.

"Was it possible?" I wondered. "Does cancer have a level of conscious control over a person that causes them to make choices that will help the disease?"

The thought was as equally insane as it was terrifying to me as I imagined a parasite living inside my dad, feeding on his organs and controlling his thoughts, actions, and speech. *Maybe cancer was a physical manifestation of a spiritual parasite*, I thought. I couldn't shake the idea, and my intuitive senses burned whenever I tried to deny what I was feeling.

Hospice

In late May of 2013, after multiple trips to the hospital, we brought my father home for the final time. He had suffered multiple strokes of varying degrees, and with each one he endured, we lost another piece of him. During the first few days on hospice, he'd have a few moments of lucidity. He'd make the occasional joke and smile at us, still convinced that he was going to get better.

He lost his ability to speak after about 4 days but could still nod his head to let us know he could understand us. We had him comfortably resting on a borrowed hospital bed in the front sunroom. He was so proud of that room, as he and a friend converted it from a screened porch to a heated family room that maximized sunlight. The room housed several Christmas mornings, late night dance-parties, and countless laughs.

The sunroom was connected to our kitchen via a set of glass sliding doors. One evening, while my dad was quietly resting, I was sitting at the kitchen table grabbing a bite to eat. My mom, brother, and I had been taking shifts sitting with him so he was never alone. My back was to him, but he was only 10 feet from where I was sitting. I was focused on ingesting my plate of scrambled eggs as fast as I could, when I sensed my father walking behind me. In my mind, I felt him get up, walk past me, and down the hall toward his bedroom.

I quickly turned around, only to see he was still resting quietly in the bed. Being exhausted, I assumed it was my imagination and I went back to my eggs. For the next 2 days, however, I kept sensing that my father was getting out of bed and walking around the house. It felt so real, as if someone was actually behind me that I expected to see him standing over me whenever I would turn around.

The next afternoon, as I was sitting by his bedside, I started asking him questions. I started by asking him if he wanted anything, and he shook his head "no." I asked if he could hear me okay, and he shook his head "yes." I asked him to blink his eyes, and he responded immediately by blinking. He was still conscious and able to understand me.

"Dad," I started, "are you having dreams?"

He turned his head toward me and nodded sternly, locking his eyes with mine.

"Are you dreaming that you are walking around the house?" I asked. He again nodded, holding my gaze.

I knew his body was preparing to let go. "I've felt you walking around, Dad. I don't think they're dreams," I explained.

Relying on my limited knowledge of out of body states and the research of Robert Monroe, I tried to alleviate any fears my dad might have had. "It's perfectly natural to have these experiences, Dad. I've had very similar dreams as well. Don't be afraid of them."

He again looked at me and nodded his head before going back to sleep.

That night, while I was trying to grab a few hours of sleep in another room, I was jolted awake to my mother screaming my name.

"Dennis!" she shouted, sounding horrified. There was another noise coming from the porch as well: a shaking sound, with grunts and moans.

I came running to find my mother standing by my father's bedside, holding onto his left arm. She was calm, but the color had drained from her face. My father was having a full grand mal seizure. His body wretched and twisted in every direction. His back arched and his legs kicked. I grabbed his other arm, and it was cool, clammy, and tense, locked in a rigid torment. His eyes rolled in all directions, and he had an uncontrollable groan that was forced from his lungs with each rapid thrust of his convulsing body.

That first seizure lasted for about 3 minutes, and when it was over, his body went limp. The left side of his face drooped from his last stroke, and he balled his right hand into a fist. He looked into my eyes and clenched his teeth as he tried to catch his breath. Only the right side of his mouth opened and as he puffed air in and out of his mouth, his right cheek puffing and deflating like a balloon.

As my father stared at me, I saw a horrible sense of anger. I saw a fear that I had never before witnessed, and I saw frustration and utter defeat. I saw my father's realization that he was dying, and a total lack of understanding as to why. Up until then, he believed he was going to live, but in that moment he was forced to face a horrid reality. His death was coming, and it would not be an easy transition.

About a week later, my father was still clinging to life. Emaciated and barely breathing, he lay in the sunroom: quiet and unresponsive as his body shut down. He hadn't eaten in almost 2 weeks, and the only water he was getting for at least a week was the occasional wet sponge we'd try to force into his mouth. They say the human body can't survive for more than 3 days without water. My father, however, suffered for much longer.

On or around June 10th, we were startled by a loud and repetitive crashing sound. It wasn't coming from within our home, but was definitely close by. On edge, I ran outside prepared for something violent, and pinpointed the source of the sounds.

The home next to us was abandoned and had been for quite some time. Yet it sounded as if something was inside, and it was trying to get out. The source of the metallic reverberations was coming from the garage door. With each eruption of furious sound, I envisioned a wild bear trapped in the garage and at any moment I expected it to tear through the thin door and come rushing at me, hungry for blood. Our fear mounted as the sound continued and intensified while my father lay just a few feet away, dying in his borrowed hospital bed.

We called our local security office, and they came to investigate. They cautiously entered the residence, and discovered not a vicious trapped bear, but a faulty electric-garage-door opener. Something kept triggering the door to open, but it was physically locked and unable to rise. As a result, the door shook viciously whenever it tried to lift. Every few hours, for the next few days during my father's transition, the garage would erupt in a series of angry clangs and bashes as it tried to free itself and open up to the world. The odd thing is, once my father passed, the garage fell silent and never made a sound again. Years later, a new resident purchased the home and my mom had a chance to speak with him. After a year in the home, not once did he recall ever having an issue with the garage door which left me wondering if the energy trying to escape the garage through a barrage of shaking was somehow connected to the seizures my father suffered as he tried to exit his physical body.

On the night of June 15th, 2013, I was again awoken to my mother screaming for me. "Dennis!" she yelled, as I came running out to find my father having another grand mal seizure. His arms were swinging wildly as his body shook in violent spasms. His eyes remained open and I grabbed his arm to protect them from hitting the metal bedrails. After about 3 minutes, the seizure stopped. At this point, the whole family was present: My brother Michael and his girlfriend Casey, my mother, and my wife Jenny all sat by his bedside. And then he started to scream…

It was the sound of raw helplessness and torture, and we were powerless to stop it. My dad roared in a torment of pain and suffering.

He'd stop momentarily to catch his breath, and then resume his bellowing. I saw panic and pain on his face, and the once vibrant, humorous man I had grown to love was no longer there. He screamed for almost an hour, as we sat there helplessly watching. I begged him to let go, but his screaming only intensified.

"He's having strokes," my mother gasped. "He's stroking out."

We sat with him until the screaming subsided, helpless to do anything but watch. Exhausted, I got up and walked into the kitchen for a moment, where I froze. For an instant, the world faded away from me, and I witnessed a familiar scene in my mind.

It was a scene from the movie Full Metal Jacket depicting the conflict in Vietnam. One of the Marines was walking between a few buildings when he was shot in the leg by a sniper. He screamed out in fear and pain, not so differently from the screams my father had just emitted. His squad watched helplessly from behind another building, feeling powerless to save him from the bullets of the vicious sniper - much like my family and I sat helplessly next to my screaming father.

Frightened and angry, they argued over what to do next.

"I think we're being set up for an ambush," the squad leader shouted. "That sniper's just trying to suck us in one at a time." He was ordering his squad to stand down and leave the wounded man exposed until support could arrive to flush out the sniper. Whenever he would try to explain the situation, however, the sniper would take another shot at the injured Marine lying in the mud, forcing another round of painful shouts and despair. Not being able to handle the screams any longer, another Marine ran out to rescue him only to feel the hot sting of yet another non-fatal wound leaving 2 suffering victims to draw in the others.[28]

There was panic on the young men's faces as they scrambled to find a way to put a stop to the torture. They were afraid, and they felt powerless to help their dying friends.

This entire scene flashed through my mind with all the pressures of an intuitive message. Although the scene seemed random, I somehow knew exactly what it was trying to tell me. As if finding the key that unlocked this mystery, the realization of this

---

[28] Kubrick, S; "et al" (Producers), Kubric, S, (Director) (1987) Full Metal Jacket (Motion Picture), United States

message released a thought:

It's after all of you, and it wants your emotions.

It was the same thought-voice that appeared months prior, encouraging me to change my diet to the potentially life-saving Alkaline Diet. Now it was warning me that something was in play around my father. I explored my feelings deeper to understand the message and realized what I needed to do.

If this spiritual sniper that was causing my father such pain was after my emotions, I knew the only way to avoid the ambush was to keep my emotions under control. I knew the vision meant I needed to stay positive, to actually *feel* love and happiness in my heart during my father's awful transition, and not just think about it. I had to let go of my fear, and focus on all of the happy memories I had of my father and try to bring that level of love to that dark scene we were all facing. I felt it would somehow offer protection to my father, and allow him to pass peacefully. If something wanted my emotional outputs of fear and sadness, I was going to do everything I could to produce the complete opposite.

I grabbed the proof copy of my memoir, *Service*, and started reading my father a chapter called "Family." It highlighted what a wonderful dad he was, and how proud I was of everything he had taught me. I read him that chapter as my brother stood at his feet with his eyes closed in meditation. My mom sat by his head, kissing him as the tears streamed down her face.

"I wasn't ready for this," she said between gasping sobs. "I'm not ready. I thought I had more time..." Her statement hung in the air heavily as she tried to grasp the fact that she needed to say goodbye to the love of her life.

None of us were ready, but I refused to allow the sadness to consume me in that moment. I was not going to rush blindly into the snipers emotional trap and fall victim to such chaos.

When I finished reading, I started telling my father stories about our life. I shared memories from our childhood and told him how thankful I was. I pulled the feelings of happiness and love from those memories into my heart and felt my sadness pushed aside. I surrounded my father and I with those wonderful feelings and memories, as he fought through his painfully slow transition.

They won't get me, I said to myself, believing that there was a spiritual sniper using my father's transition as an opportunity to draw in more victims for a rampage of suffering. *I know you now*, I thought, *and you will not get me.*

For the next two to three hours, my father's breathing was incredibly labored. With each exhale, he let out a slight groan, and fell into a delayed, but steady rhythm. The time between each breath grew greater to the point where he was getting one gasp of air every minute - yet he still held on.

Just after midnight on June 13, 2013, my first Father's Day, I stepped outside to get some air. My mom and brother went to use the bathroom, Jenny went to check on my son, and Casey sat by Dad's side to talk to him. The hospice nurse joined me out front, and we talked about giving my father more morphine to make him comfortable.

"You know," she said, "at this point, you really can't give him too much."

I froze for a moment, absorbing the weight of what she had just said. I wanted to end his suffering, but being just moments away from an actual opportunity to commit to such a task, I didn't know if I had the strength to carry it out. I walked back inside, looking to consult my family. Casey was still with him as he lay motionless, staring at the ceiling.

"Dad?" I said, as I walked closer to him and placed my hand on his chest. It was stiff and still. I waited a minute longer. The room felt lighter. No more forced breathing. No more groans. He was gone.

"He's gone," I said loud enough for everyone to hear.

My family flooded into the room, as he lay there breathless. My father, a wonderfully funny, loving, and happy man, was dead.

The death certificate would falsely read lung cancer. A day after his transition, the second opinion from another doctor came back and said pancreatic cancer. There was no mention of a parasite. No mention of something taking over my fathers mind. There was no mention of the spiritual sniper, but one wouldn't expect to find reference to such horrible monsters in the documents, diagnoses, and opinions of our trusted medical and scientific experts. Such parasitic creatures capable of

manipulating the human mind and behaviors
don't exist.

Or do they?

Who's in Control?

One of the things that bothered me most about my father's passing was his refusal to ingest foods that would have helped to save or at least prolong his life. I couldn't understand why he would refuse to even try to drink a simple smoothie each day, even if it tasted bad or made him nauseous, knowing that by rejecting such nourishment he was minimizing his chances for survival.

I kept envisioning a parasite inside my father, manipulating his choices and controlling his behavior. Was it even possible for a parasite to take control of all or part of its host's decision-making abilities, even if such choices would knowingly lead to the ultimate demise of the host? Are we really that vulnerable? Once again, in an attempt to understand the world around me, I set my attention on nature and started my research into the abusive world of parasitism. What I found presented the cycle of life in a horrifying new light.

Drug Addicts

In the tropical forests of Central America, the thorny, nectar-filled Acacia Trees have recruited the protection of a tiny, but vengeful bodyguard. Known commonly as the Acacia Ant, this species makes its home in the hollow thorns of the Acacia Tree.

These soldier-ants constantly patrol the branches and leaves of their home and will immediately engage and attack any threats to the tree. If a creeping vine starts to curl its way onto the Acacia, the ants will use their powerful jaws to chomp through the vine, freeing their home from the invasive, sun-blocking and restrictive species. If another insect attempts to build its home within the tree, these warrior-ants go to war defending their home.[29]

In exchange for their protection, the tree provides small nodes throughout that secrete nectar, which is the food source of the ants. This gift of food from the tree, however, comes with a captivatingly high price.

---

[29] Yong, E. (2013, November 6) Trees Trap Ants into Sweet Servitude. Retrieved from http://news.nationalgeographic.com/news/2013/11/131106-ants-tree-acacia-food-mutualism/

In order to survive, the Acacia Ants need to ingest sucrose, a type of sugar, as a part of their diet. In order to digest sucrose, however, the ants must produce an enzyme called invertase, which aids in the breakdown of the sucrose into smaller, digestible sugars. [29]

Although normally produced by ants, "(i)n 2005, Martin Heil (of Cinvestav Unidad Irapuato in Mexico), showed that all of the workers of the Acacia Ant lack invertase activity and cannot digest normal sources of sucrose." The Acacia Tree, however, generously compensates for the ants' deficit by secreting it into its nectar. What's interesting is that, according to Heil, ant larvae are born with the ability to produce invertase, but upon reaching adulthood, that ability is deactivated by the Acacia Tree. 29 above

When the adult ant emerges from its nest for the first time, it will make its way to one of the nectar nodules on the tree where it will indulge its first meal. What Heil discovered was that the nectar produced by the Acacia, which flows freely from the nodules for the ants to consume, contains chitinase enzymes. [29]

Chitinase enzymes irreversibly disable the ants' ability to produce invertase and therefore destroy the ants' ability to digest sugars other than the one produced by the Acacia Tree. The Acacia, through the use of the chitinase enzymes, manipulates the ants' digestive systems to the point that the only food they are able to process is that which is provided by the Acacia.[29]

In essence, the tree has created a seemingly welcoming environment for the ants, offering them shelter and food. Once they ingest the food, however, the tree alters the ants so the Acacia's nectar is the only food the ants are capable of consuming. This leaves the ants no choice but to defend and protect the tree in order to maintain their food source and enslavement.

Zombies

Creating nectar-addicted servants as a private security force is not Nature's only mechanism of control. The Emerald Cockroach Wasp (Ampulex Compressa) possesses a different approach to domineering its victim, using a combination of stealth, violence, and brain surgery.

With a beautiful hue of metallic blue-green, this elegant creature carefully makes her way across the ground in search of her much larger prey. Stalking her unsuspecting victim, she crawls behind it undetected, waiting for her moment to pounce. When the time is right, she strikes with a stinging precision, targeting and disabling the roach's front legs. Unable to escape, the victim can't fight back as the wasp administers her second strike: a much more delicate injection deep into the roach's brain, flooding it with her mind-controlling neurotoxin.[30]

The venom disables the cockroach's desire to escape, and she pauses momentarily to allow the toxin to take affect. After a moment, she surgically removes a piece of the roach's antenna and sips some of its blood, possibly gauging if the dose of the venom was appropriate. As the wasp drinks from the antenna, the roach does not move, and makes no attempt to resist. [30]

The wasp takes hold of the roach's other antenna and delicately guides it to her

[30] Team Candiru (User Name). (2015 April 18) Beautiful Wasp Zombifies Cockroach. (Video) Retrieved from https://www.youtube.com/watch?v=-ySwuQhruBo

burrow like an obedient dog on a leash. The roach follows willingly and makes no attempt to get away as it is led into the dark depths of the wasps waiting burrow.[30]

Once inside, the roach lay motionless as the wasp begins caressing its belly with her backside, searching for the perfect location to lay her precious egg with a deadly package waiting to emerge. Delicately, she attaches her egg to the belly of the roach and then exits the burrow, sealing the entrance shut with rocks and dirt. The roach lay motionless in the darkness, making no attempt to exit, as the larva prepares to emerge.[30]

As the young wasp-larva hatches, it slowly bores its way into the soft belly of the motionless, but still very-much-alive roach. It begins to eat, moving through the roach's soft insides, consuming the internal organs yet taking care to avoid those necessary to keep the roach alive. [30]

It's a slow death, as the growing larva eats its way through the roach's softness, until finally, it reaches maturity as it tears its way out of the hollow roach carcass, up through the burrow, and into the world in search of its next victim to hypnotize, infect, and consume....

God's Parasites are a Natural Part of this World

Parasitic relationships exist all throughout nature – with the tiny parasite infecting the mind of its victims, controlling them to the point of suicide in order to promote the lifecycle of the parasite.

Pill bugs ingest parasites through the bird droppings they consume. The parasites then manipulate the bug to expose itself to predators, ultimately committing suicide by being eaten. When a bird eats the suicidal bug, the life cycle of the parasite begins anew – leaving more offspring in the droppings to be consumed by the next generation of pillbug victims.[31]

There is a species of carpenter ant that falls prey to a particular fungus. It bores its way into the ants brain, forcing it to leave its colony and perch itself on the underside of a leaf. The fungus consumes the entire body, and eventually produces a stalk through the head of the ant, which will burst spores onto the ground below, waiting for future prey to continue the cycle of control, death, and rebirth.[31]

Nature, it seems, is not always the loving and peaceful energy we may believe her to be. She can be cunning, cruel, and ruthless, allowing for the torturous and painful death of many forms of life on this planet. Life requires death – in order for something to live, something else must die. In many cases, that death is painful and frightening for the victims.

These parasites, it seems, take killing to a much darker level. What's concerning is that such darkness seems to be a natural part of the cycle of life on this planet, and it leaves

---

[31] Gammon, K. (2012, September 7). *Zombie Bugs: 5 Real Life Cases of Body Snatching.* Retrieved from https://www.livescience.com/34196-zombie-animals.html

me wondering about the design of life. If life was intelligently designed by a divine creator, then what does this design of predation and parasitism tell us about that creator?

As humans, we often feel we are chosen, or special in the eyes of God. But are we? If life was intelligently designed, and humans are special, does that mean we are exempt from such cruelty? Can a parasite gain control of a human mind to manipulate our behavior? Was my father's personality being manipulated when he would refuse the healthy food we'd prepare for him to help fight the cancer? Was there intelligence behind his cancer that was influencing his self-destructive behavior? If so, what benefit could be gained by a parasite from his slow, painful death?

After my father died, I began searching for answers. I wanted to see if there were documented cases of parasites affecting human behavior, and to my surprise, there are:

According to the CDC, "Toxoplasma gondi is a protozoan parasite that infects most species of warm-blooded animals, including humans, and can cause the disease toxoplasmosis."

The CDC goes onto explain that T.gondi must inhabit domestic cats in order to complete its life cycle. However, it has also infected a vast multitude of other species.[32]

The life cycle of T. gondi originates within the intestines of the domestic cat. It is excreted through the feces, where it can then contaminate local water, soil, and plant life. The soil, water, and plant material containing T. gondii are then consumed by small creatures like birds and rodents. Once in an intermediate host, T. gondii forms cysts in the neural and muscular tissue. When the intermediate host is eventually consumed by another cat, the life-cycle can again continue. Animals bred for human consumption are not immune, and therefore humans can also become infected by ingesting an intermediate host with the cysts formed by T. gondii. [32]

Once inside the human body, the parasites again form cysts, "most commonly in skeletal muscle, myocardium, brain, and eyes; these cysts may remain throughout the life of the host."[32]

---

[32] Centers for Disease Control and Prevention (2018, September 5). *Parasites – Toxoplasmosis (Toxoplasma Infection)* Retreived from https://www.cdc.gov/parasites/toxoplasmosis/biology.html

These cysts alter the behavior of the hosts, causing them to increase their risk-taking behavior, and in some cases, commit suicide.

In a paper titled "Fatal attraction in rats infected with Toxoplasma gondii," it states:

…(A)lthough rats have evolved anti-predator avoidance of areas with signs of cat presence, T. gondii's manipulation appears to alter the rat's perception of cat predation risk, in some cases turning their innate aversion into an imprudent attraction. The selectivity of such behavioral changes suggests that this ubiquitous parasite subtly alters the brain of its intermediate host to enhance predation rate whilst leaving other behavioral categories and general health intact.[33]

Therefore, the infected rats are more likely to expose themselves to predation because consumption by a cat would allow the parasite to continue its lifecycle. According to the above paper, both rats with a T. gondii infection and those without were exposed to the odor of cat urine. The study found that

[33] Bedroy, M., Webster, J., & Macdonald, D. (1998, October 10). Fatal Attraction in Rats Infected with Toxoplasma Gondii. *The Royal Society* (PDF) Retreived from https://www.ncbi.nlm.nih.gov/pmc/articles/PMC1690701/pdf/11007336.pdf

"(e)ven naïve laboratory rats that have not been in contact with cats for several hundred generations still show strong aversive reactions when confronted with cat odors." Those rats that were infected with T. gondii, however, "tend to exhibit a preference for predator-scented areas," thereby are increasing their chances of being consumed by a cat.[33]

In humans, the parasite seems to enact a similar level of manipulation:

In one laboratory experiment, human dendritic cells were infected with toxoplasma. After infection, the cells, which are a key component of the immune defense, started secreting the signal substance GABA. In another experiment on live mice, the team was able to trace the movement of infected dendritic cells in the body after introducing the parasite into the brain, from where it spread and continued to affect the GABA system.[34]

GABA is a signal substance that, amongst

---

[34] Karolinska Institutet (2012, December 6). How Common 'Cat Parasite' Gets into Human Brain and Influences Human Behavior. *ScienceDaily* Retrieved From https://www.sciencedaily.com/releases/2012/12/12120620324 0.htm

other effects, inhibits the sensation of fear and anxiety. Disturbances of the GABA system are seen in people with depression, schizophrenia, bipolar diseases, anxiety syndrome, and other mental diseases.[34]

In other words, T. gondii is able to switch off the centers of the brain that respond to fear and anxiety, which could influence a person to take greater risks. Much like the rat that no longer fears the scent of cat urine, the human may no longer fear doing things that could result in the loss of life or cause a variety of other mental-health issues.

Parasites are a part of the natural order of the world we live in. They infect all forms of life, and have demonstrated the ability to influence thought and behavior. I continued to wonder if my father's mind was somehow infected with a parasitic force. Was cancer acting as an intelligent parasite, forcing my father to reject the foods that would have helped improve his condition? Was it causing him to lose his temper and argue with his family?

In a 2010 study from Binghamton University, it was hypothesized that "exposure to a directly transmitted human pathogen-flu virus-increases human social behavior presymptomatically." The study found that "(h)uman social behavior does, indeed, change with exposure. Compared to the 48 hours pre-exposure, participants interacted with significantly more people, and in significantly larger groups, during the 48 hours immediately post-exposure."[35]

One can assume that if the flu is influencing people to socialize more once infected, it is in order to spread the virus to others. Does this denote a level of intelligence in the virus itself? Or a program that is being carried out by the virus? What about cancer? What benefit does cancer gain by causing a person to resist something that will help cure the cancer? It may grow stronger in the interim, but if the host dies, so does the cancer.

Does cancer simply want the host to expire? Or was something else taking advantage of my father's weakened state, influencing his poor decisions to promote more stress, anxiety, and suffering? This is a question to which I have yet to find an answer. Lastly, is

---

[35] Reiber, C. Et. Al. (2010, October 20). Change in Human Social Behavior in Response to Common Vaccine. *Annals of Epidemiology* Retreived from https://www.ncbi.nlm.nih.gov/pubmed/20816312

it possible that many of us are currently infected by parasites? Are we being manipulated to perform certain tasks or behaviors that will somehow benefit these parasites? Whether we are or not, one thing is certain:

Monsters are real...

Animal Cruelty

Life on this planet requires death. We are all consumers of life, and in order to sustain our own life force, we must ingest the energy of another. We may not be parasites infecting the brains of other forms, but we are predators responsible for the deaths of millions, if not billions, of creatures on this planet. We corral them, confine them, and torture them. We slaughter them carelessly, allowing their companions to suffer the screams of their dying kin. We lie to ourselves in our beliefs that these creatures lack feelings and understanding of their plight, and convince ourselves that these beautiful creatures are somehow inferior to humanity and our superior cravings.

Some members of our society have decided to boycott such cruelty, and consume only plant-based foods and products. But after reading the studies of Cleve Backster who demonstrated a measurable reaction among plants when harm was inflicted upon them or other life forms in their vicinity, does it really matter? If plants are in fact emotional beings, is there a difference between the suffering of a plant and the suffering of a pig or a cow? In the end, it seems that no matter what choice is made, life was designed to elicit suffering and fear in order for life to survive. With the requirement for life to consume life on this planet, what does that tell us about our purpose and our role in the food chain? What does that tell us about ourselves?

As humans, we often live in a world of intentional ignorance. Most of us no longer slaughter the food we eat and are removed from the systematic daily process of death and cruelty committed against our animal brethren as they are prepared for consumption. We choose to avoid this routine, and therefore have no remorse or respect for the lives that were lost in honor of our own nourishment. Through our removal from this process, we have allowed for the perpetual suffering of billions on this planet.

We must remember, however, that we have a

measurable connection to all life on Earth through the electromagnetic field generated from our heart. With this field, we can commune through our emotions, but through the nullification of this sense we have lost our contact with Nature. We have silenced our abilities to hear her cries for mercy. Nature, however, has never stopped talking to us. It is we who have stopped listening, drowning out her pleas with the groans of a hungry stomach awaiting its next meal.

Perceptions may change, however, if we one day found ourselves to be the victims of such cruelty; if we were to realize that in the shadows of our ignorance lurked a predator, one that viewed us much the same way we view livestock: as a proprietary source of nourishment; an object to be cultivated, corralled, and harvested. If we were to realize this possibility, we may change the manner in which we obtain our food.

This predator is a parasite, and like the ants of the acacia, we have become drunk with its potion. We have become as the roach injected by the wasp - calmly trapped in her burrow, being slowly consumed for our energy in the darkness of our own ignorance. The farmers are among us: we are their cattle and they are *hungry…*

And always, night and day, he was in the mountains, and in the tombs, crying and cutting himself with stones. But when he saw Jesus afar off, he ran and worshipped him, And cried with a loud voice, and said, What have I to do with thee, Jesus, thou Son of the most high God? I adjure thee by God, that thou torment me not.

For he said unto him, Come out of the man, thou unclean spirit. And he asked him, What is thy name? And he answered, saying, My name is Legion: for we are many.

And he besought him much that he would not send them away out of the country. Now there was there nigh unto the mountains a great herd of swine feeding. And all the devils besought him, saying, Send us into the swine, that we may enter into them. And forthwith Jesus gave them leave. And the unclean spirits went out, and entered into the swine: and the herd ran violently down a steep place into the sea, (they were about two thousand;) and were choked in the sea. (Mark 5, 5 – 13)

Paralysis

1996.

It was late, and I found myself straddling the realms of waking life and the dream world. The softness of my comforter enveloped me like a cloud as the mellow green glow from my alarm clock lightly filled the room. I contemplated getting out of bed to get a snack, but realized that remaining in the protective warmth of my bed was a much better idea.

I went to roll over to check the time, when my entire body was shocked into a rigid state of paralysis. Flat on my back and frozen in place, I struggled to bring air into my lungs. My chest heaved upwards as I frantically sucked air through my nose, which felt more like a tightly pinched straw.

Seconds dripped by like hours, and a

growing rage of panic exploded all around me. My mind was consumed with breath and movement, both which seemed to be eluding me. Then, just at the edge of my periphery, I noticed something. A shadow. I couldn't quite see it, but felt it was there, standing over me, watching me struggle. It had a heavy, menacing presence and my awareness of it seemed to magnify the fear inside of me. Something was in my room, and it was moving closer to me.

I started to scream, but all that escaped from my vocal cords was a light rasping sound as air forced its way through my frozen throat. Then suddenly and without warning, a hand reached out and rested firmly on my chest, piercing the veil between dream and reality. The touch held the heavy weight of physicality and removed all possibility that this was a dream. It had density, and through the physical sensation of touch I knew it had power over me. It had taken control of my body and was influencing my feelings and mind. I knew it wanted me to be afraid, and I believed there was nothing I could do to stop it. My urgent panic of resistance surged with this electrifying validation of reality, when suddenly - an overwhelming desire to sleep overcame me. My panic ceased, as did my resistance, and I fell into a deep and unknowing sleep.

I awoke the next morning and sat up. The warmth of the sun streamed through my window as tiny flecks of dust danced lazily in the light. I sat there for a moment, trying to remember the night before. There was a fog covering my mind, and the harder I tried to see what was hidden, the thicker the fog became. I could see the memory drifting further and further away from me, and no matter how deeply I focused, I just couldn't catch it. I paused for a moment, and then remembered that hand on my chest.

It happened. I thought. *It was standing next to my bed and it touched me. This is real.* As the realization burst into my mind, doubt immediately followed. *Maybe it was a dream*, I thought. *Maybe.*

I encountered these visitations frequently when I was younger and found the immediate onset of fear to be a common thread. My paralysis magnified my horror. I was unable to move or scream, and despite being in a blinding rage of terror, I'd suddenly decide it was a good idea to go back to sleep. No matter how hard I tried, whenever one of these creatures would appear, I'd suffer in fear for a few moments and then fall fast asleep. I had no control over my body and fought to control my own mind. As a trained police officer and soldier, I have never given up in battle, and certainly have never felt the need to go to sleep in the face of fear. I have an intimate relationship with my fear and have developed the ability to compartmentalize it so I can surgically dissect the finest details in a violent situation. Going to sleep is counterintuitive to all of my training and experience and not something I would ever consider doing on my own. I suspect that whoever these visitors are, they have the ability to not only influence my emotional state, but also induce me into a state of slumber.

Do these beings have the ability to possess the human body? As stated in Mark 5 (above), the possessed man was often seen crying and cutting himself with stones. The reader is led to believe he was under the direct influence of the Legion of spirits inhabiting his body. Were they forcing him to cut himself? Did my nightly encounters with these creatures involve a similar mechanism to control my own body and mind? Is such a relationship even possible? In studying the habits of parasites, nature has taught us that possession of one's mind, body, and behavior is a very real, and very common occurrence. The question then comes to rise, who, or what, are these figures that take control in the night?

Control

In 2005, about a year after my return from my military deployment to Bosnia, I found myself struggling to assimilate back into civilian life. I felt disconnected from the world, and as a result, Ashley, my fiancé at the time, and I were growing apart. I was falling into a deep depression as I tried to make sense of my life. I feared working a 9 – 5 job and worried that the only things I'd have to look forward to in life would be the end of the workweek and the start of the weekend. I was saddened by the redundant cycle that so many people I knew were a part of: Go to work, come home, look forward to the weekend, get drunk, dread Monday, and go back to work. Unfortunately, I felt myself being sucked into the cycle, and was standing on the line of submission, almost willing to accept my defeat and give in because I saw no other alternative.

I was trying to make sense of the world after spending 10 months immersed in the conflicting arena of counterintelligence and terrorism. I was trying to conform based on my training, but had other spiritual interests that didn't fit with the way the world was supposed to work. I felt different, and a little crazy inside, and Ashley was happy to reaffirm my sentiments by telling me how weird I was for my interest in spiritual and supernatural topics. Those topics, however, were the only things that brought me comfort. There was something about my research into the unknown that drove me and made me feel alive inside. I was trying to discover my purpose in life, and figure out who I really was. I believed that that with each article or book I read I'd be one step closer to finding some much-needed answers.

In July 2004, I purchased a home for Ashley and me. Where I had once had aspirations of a prosperous career in intelligence with the federal government, I now had aspirations of getting drunk on the weekends and working for the sole purpose of paying my bills. I had hoped that buying a home would bring us closer together, however, I soon began to suspect there were greater forces working to drive us apart.

Over the next year, we spoke less and fought more frequently. I was berated regularly by Ashley, and eventually came to believe the condescending things she was saying about me.

"You're such a fucking loser. You're no fun. You don't know how to relax. You always think something bad is going to happen, but it never does. What's the matter with you?"

I felt like a failure and I was embarrassed about my life. I was in a constant state of emotional suffering, and it was completely exhausting. I withdrew from friends and family, and found myself feeling alone and seeking solitude.

At some point during this time, a strange concept came to me. I didn't pay much attention to the message at first and assumed it was a rogue thought running through my mind.

They are using her to come after you.

The thought continued and would pop into

my mind randomly, and I had no idea what it meant or why I was thinking it. As it repeated and I began to contemplate it's meaning, I came to believe that for some reason *they* could not get to me. I'm not sure why, but I assumed *they* were somehow connected to the dark presence that paralyzed me in the night.

I searched my intuition and gained the feeling that for reasons unknown to me, they couldn't affect me the way they wanted to. As a countermeasure, they began using Ashley to get to me instead. I began to suspect they manipulated her to break me down, weaken me, and create vulnerability.

Over time, she began to change. She was a different person from the girl I first met, and a certain heaviness seemed to fill the room whenever we were together. Her words were cruel, and our conversations often left me feeling embarrassed, incompetent, and alone.

They're using her to get to you.

One night as we were getting ready to go out, Ashley was in the shower while I was doing some reading on the computer. I craved opportunities to do research, but never knew exactly what I was looking for. It was just a deep-rooted feeling that would direct my searches to various esoteric and occult subjects. Sometimes, this draw was so powerful that I half-expected to receive a package containing a cell phone and a call from Morpheus to tell me the Matrix was real and I was trapped inside. That night, I was about halfway through an article about the occult when Ashley came out of the shower, wrapped in a towel.

"What are you reading?" she asked. Her tone was angry and abrupt.

"It's an article about the occult and history of religion," I said excitedly. "I really think-"

"I swear to God you're the weirdest fucking person I know. You and your mom are the only two people who are into all that alien stuff. You're never going to figure anything out. You're so fucking weird."

"Don't you want to know who we are and where we come from?" I asked her, pleading for mercy.

"You're never going to figure it out," she coldly restated and then walked away.

I felt defeated. I stopped reading and shut off the computer. I was embarrassed to search for answers on the only subject that gave me peace in my own home.

Maybe they really are using her to get to me…

It seemed that my inquiry into spirituality really set her off, so maybe there was a connection between my search and them. But then again, maybe I was just crazy. In July 2005, however, the tension between us became unbearable. I despised my own existence as I slowly drowned in the meager and shameful life I had allowed to engulf me. It was a cold, dead feeling that left only the faintest memory of the confident soldier I once was. Not knowing if I had the mental strength to fight off the suicidal thoughts that were beginning to infect my mind, I asked Ashley to leave. It was the only chance I had of emerging from the darkness that now flooded my home and my thoughts. I needed to get away from her and the negative gas that seemed to stalk me in her presence.

Our breakup was anything but easy. She yelled at me, she insulted me, and then she began to beg me. Almost everyday for the next six months she came by. We'd talk, we'd cry, and she'd ask if she could stay. I don't know how I was able to turn her away each day because with each rejection I offered her, I sank deeper into a state of self-loathing. I contemplated taking her back just to stop the remorse I felt each time I had to tell her no; it was so bothersome that I began to indulge in wondering if I'd be better off dead.

They're using her to get to you.

One afternoon, Ashley was at the house. We were standing in the kitchen and talking. I took note of just how sweet she was being toward me, and how beautiful she looked. During our conversation, I began to wonder if I should give into her requests and allow her another chance to make things right. As I pondered this, however, I noticed something strange. Just over her right shoulder, almost directly behind her, there was a shadow. This shadow was not on the wall but was floating in the air behind her. I looked away, thinking my eyes were playing tricks on me, but when I looked back it was still there and had taken the form of a human-like figure with a head and torso, about 6-feet tall. The shadow became more crisp and faded into a glowing blackness standing behind her. As this form stood uncomfortably close to her, she again asked me to take her back.

"But I waited for you all that time while you were away," she pleaded, striking my strongest chord of guilt over the breakup.

"I don't think things are going to work," I forced myself to say. The guilt was starting to overtake me and I wanted to run away screaming with a hatred for myself, but couldn't stop staring at this floating black shadow-thing behind her. Then, in a rapid sequence as if a broken record was skipping in my mind, a flurry of thoughts emerged:

I am such an asshole! She waited for you and this is how you repay her?! I hate myself! Doesn't she deserve another chance, you piece of shit!??

My thoughts shouted at me all at once and repeated themselves over and over as if they were independent entities themselves. I fought to regain control of my mind:

What is that shadow standing behind her? I wondered, and suddenly my thoughts began to slow. Deep down I felt a sense of knowing, and with that knowing came a momentary sense of calm. This knowing started in the center of my chest and flowed throughout my entire body. It was as if my heart was thinking in terms of feelings, and my brain was then interpreting those feelings into words that I could logically understand.

"It is using her to come after you," the feeling told me.

At realizing this thought, I stood up straight and stepped back. Although weak, I felt a hint of my moral courage return. I glanced at Ashley but could no longer see the blackness floating behind her.

"Ashley, I just don't think this is going to work," I calmly explained.

There were more tears, and once again, she left my home. I felt exhausted and wanted desperately to run to her car and beg her to stay because of the pain I knew I was causing her. But I couldn't forget what I saw behind her.

They are using her to get to you.

Was it possible? Was there really something we failed to perceive that had infected our relationship? If so, why??? What did it want with me? What did it want with her? What the hell was that shadow?

Years later, I came across a lecture by David Icke. He was making a reference to his book The Biggest Secret about an all-too-familiar experience. When I finally had an opportunity to view the image he was referring to, I felt a sense of vindication and sanity, followed by an overwhelming shock.

In his book there was a page of several hand-drawn images of reptilian beings. The last drawing on the page was of a young boy with a large-humanoid shadow hovering behind him. The caption read:

"… (Clive) Burrows produced these illustrations from descriptions by one of the countless people I have met who see the reptiles of the lower fourth dimension. They appear to attach to humans by two of the lower chakras."[36]

That was exactly what I saw standing behind Ashley. Why was it there? Why did I see it? And more importantly, how did I know it was using her to get to me?

I witnessed this shadow behind Ashley before I saw David Icke's image. This gives me confidence that I had in-fact perceived something real, or conversely, if I am crazy and delusional, it shows me that I am not alone which also lends credence that

---

[36] Icke, David (1999, February) The Biggest Secret. Isle of Wight, UK: David Icke Books

something is happening and what I experienced is a part of the human condition. Something was coming after us. Despite its attempts to continue to pursue me, however, Ashley was gone from my life. I was left alone, depressed, and hating the man I had become. I had nothing left but an eternity of time to reflect on my thoughts and feelings, leaving me completely vulnerable to anything that preys on people in such lowly states...

Glimpses of the Farmers

Periodically throughout most of my life, I have faced imposing dark shadows in-between the worlds of wakefulness and sleep. They came in the night bringing their gifts of paralysis and fear, and provided me with raw vulnerability and helplessness.

For the majority of my life, I had no memories of their faces. What I could recall of them was extremely fragmented, and whenever I'd try to remember what they looked like, my minds eye would present a blurry shadow, sometimes showing a frail body with spindly arms, or just a mass of darkness around a formless body.

Having watched many movies and read several books on the subject of UFO encounters and alien abduction, I sometimes wondered if I was being visited by the popular large-eyed Greys who are often referenced in UFO abduction reports. But there was something different about my experiences. They seemed more dream-like than physical, but still captured an undeniable element of realness. Seeing their faces, I feared, would be traumatizing, and I worried that such an encounter would remove my ability to pretend it was all a dream and force their presence violently into my waking reality.

I wanted to know who they were, but more importantly, I needed to know what they wanted with me. It seemed the more I tried to learn about them, however, the more intense and scary my experiences became and I often wondered if they were trying to deter me from searching for answers. This idea only drove me to search with a deeper sense of urgency and determination.

When I was about 25 years old, I intensified my search with a new-sense of necessity. I no longer wanted to be alone in this journey, and decided to create a discussion forum on the Internet to connect with other experiencers like myself. I spent several hours preparing my first posting, envisioning hundreds of people coming forward to share their stories.

As I wrote down my experiences, I felt rebellious, as if my simple act of admission would spark an awakening and bring light to the existence of these terrifying shadow figures and end their reign of tyranny. I wanted to lend support to others who were fearful to sleep at night, and hoped together we could forge a plan to combat these nightly invaders. I decided I would no longer be a passive participant in this experience, and was going to pursue this event as far as I possibly could.

That night, however, I worried that my open move of inquiry would invite a deeper level of harassment from them as I cautiously drifted to sleep expecting the worst. A few hours later, the worst arrived at my bedside…

At 1:38 a.m. I awoke frazzled in a panic. I had to take a few moments to calm myself down, and when I stopped shaking, I began frantically scrawling in my journal. It was the most intense encounter I had ever experienced, and my body continued to tremble as I tried to readjust my focus to my sudden waking. Although I recognized the familiar surroundings of my bedroom, I still felt as if I was in my childhood bedroom, connected to the experience I had just endured. I felt as if I was in 2 places at the same time, bilocated between the two rooms. This sensation didn't last long, fortunately, and I eventually merged fully into the safety of my bed.

Moments before they arrived, I was somehow aware they were coming. I found that I suddenly had a precognition that allowed me to perceive a few moments into the future, and this ability only enhanced the scariness of the experience. As if on cue, three beings appeared in my room and surrounded my bed. Although my vision was blurry, through my peripherals I could see two slender, shadowy figures standing on either side of me, and one at the foot of my bed. Their presence felt heavy, as if their arrival caused the air around me to press harder on my body. It was a suffocating feeling that put me in a state of anxious anticipation, like one would feel upon realizing they were about to be attacked. This pressure seemed to emanate from them, and I felt that this was somehow intentionally directed toward me.

My body tensed with fear, which was

intensified by a sense of knowing what they were going to do moments before they did it. This anticipation added to the terror as my mind tried even harder to prevent what they were preparing to do. As a cop I often felt the scariest part of a violent encounter was the moment before it happened; the knowing that a life or death situation was about to occur and the thousands of dreadful thoughts that accompanied that knowing. With this brief precognition of their intentions, my mind raced to explore what could happen, which resulted in even more terrifying scenarios of possibility. Something awful was pending, and I was not prepared for it. I knew what they were going to do; I knew what they were going to allow me to see, but I was not ready.

Then, as if on cue, out of the darkness came the clarity of their three faces. The shadows melted away and the blurriness burst into focus. Never before had I seen their faces during an encounter, and nothing prepared me for such grotesque hideousness. They were troll-like and smooshed, with a dark brownish-grey color. Their lips had deep creases around them that gave their face a downward-looking draw. They looked like angry little hairless apes, and possessed a sense of power and control. As they forced me to absorb their images, I remember thinking: *Oh God I've got the ugly ones!* and somehow understood that to mean that this particular breed did not have my best intentions in mind.

These creatures did not have the sleek-smooth skin of the popular Greys, whose faces seemed to pop up everywhere from bumper stickers to t-shirts. Had the faces of these trolls been made popular, I think every man, woman, and child in the world would be afflicted with nightmares. To stare at them was to intimately face a horrifying terror. To stare at them was to know fear – to absorb it, taste it, and be consumed by it. These were real monsters, and it was quite clear they wanted to scare me. There was no mind reading and no body language – just an intimately raw communication of harsh intention and feeling. It was a transmission of fear in its purest form.

As their final gesture of intimidation, most likely to ensure the realness of the experience, their hands crossed the divide between dream-state and reality. They were all over my body; grabbing and touching, as I lay there frozen, subject to their pokes, prods, and contact. My body was stiff and rigid, frozen in place, yet my sense of touch remained intact. They wanted me to feel the realness of their touch, and I was powerless to stop them.

I was beyond my breaking point, and losing my mind to fear. My pre-cognition, however, remained clear and focused. I continued to know what was coming next, and pleaded in my mind for it to stop. They were touching my face, which felt like a final act of dominance over me. They wanted me to know they had total control over me, as if I was a helpless prisoner victim to their every desire. It was as humiliating as it was terrorizing and there was nothing left for me to do but scream.

I screamed in my own head, and my inner voice echoed throughout my mind. I screamed so hard in my mind that all thought disappeared in the shouting. Through my mental screams of panic, I tried to manifest sound through my stiff, frozen vocal cords. I have never screamed so intensely before, as this was a scream that could only birth through the purest quality of terror. I screamed rapaciously in my mind, trying desperately to force my vocal cords to open, when finally, a horrendous roar escaped in an eruption of frightful sound. It was a single belt that was so deep and so loud that I woke myself from the experience. Once awake, however, I continued to roar as if a part of me was still trapped in that bed with those trollish faces and prodding hands. I shouted so loud that I didn't realize I was the one who was screaming. It was perplexing to not only hear myself scream, but to be startled and confused by it as well. As my room faded into focus, I was able to ground myself and quiet my screams.

I sat for a moment and was amazed that they allowed me to see their faces. The instant my conscious mind drew my attention to this fact, however, the clarity of their faces went black. It was as if the file containing the memory for their faces was still there, but when I tried to open it, the data was no longer accessible. I knew that I saw their faces in perfect detail, and I knew that they looked more like trolls than Hollywood aliens, but I could no longer recall the specific features of their faces. In my mind I made a comparison to the portrayal of the beings from the popular movie *Fire in The Sky*, but knew that what I saw still looked different, uglier, and far more terrifying. Now, over 10 years later, every so often I will get the briefest of glimpses of those faces and as far as I can tell, they do resemble a type of hairless monkey. In making that comparison, I am reminded of something my younger brother Michael told me when he was just 4 years old.

"Do you remember when the bad monkeys came, Dennis?" he asked one day. "You were screaming at them to get away…"

I had no recollection of the bad monkeys, but it was something he asked me a few times in our youth. After seeing their faces in my encounter, I can't help but to wonder if these beings were the bad monkeys Michael was referring to. It's also interesting to note that this dream-state experience seemed to play out in my childhood bedroom, set around the same time period Michael first told me about

seeing the bad monkeys.

Journaling

With memory of these events being extremely difficult to hold onto, I began keeping a journal in my early twenties. In reflecting back through my experiences, I noticed similarities among my encounters. Something was happening, but I struggled to understand whether it was a physical encounter, a misunderstood manifestation of my own consciousness, a deeper spiritual encounter - equally as real as a physical one - or a combination of the mix. It was confusing the way a dream would melt into a sense of realness, or a seemingly physical encounter would take place in a strange location – yet moments later I'd awaken in my bed.

Had I not written down my experiences immediately upon waking, the majority of them may have been lost forever. Even now as I review them, they seem more like stories from someone else than personal experiences.

But they happened, and at the time of writing them they felt real.

On the pages that follow are excerpts from my journal, supported with my analysis, detailing some of my experiences with these creatures – the farmers of fear, as I have come to know them. My goal in sharing is to provide as close to a first-hand account as possible, in hopes that others can compare their experiences to mine, find commonalities, and hopefully learn enough about this experience so we can develop effective interventions and countermeasures. Through my own analysis, I believe I have learned what they want from me. As a result, I have begun to carefully craft my resistance…

Sometime in early February, 2004:

This was the start of it all. I awoke in the middle of the night to find myself standing inches in front of our bedroom closet. I was facing the door and sensed that Ashley was standing to my right. I tried to move, but felt rigid and paralyzed. I tried to scream, but my vocal cords felt as stiff and paralyzed as the rest of my body. I sensed at *least 1 to 2 beings in the room behind us, but was not able to see them. I only felt their presence behind me. It was a pressing feeling, as if their presence in the room created a pressure on my body that I could feel whenever they were around. I felt that they were taking something from us against our will. I don't know how else to explain it other than it felt like they were taking our energy or our spirituality/souls. I did not get a good feeling from these beings. Their presence felt heavy and dark and I did not believe they had my best interests in mind.*

Ashley wasn't a big believer in these things, so I was careful when I spoke to her the next morning. I simply asked if she had any funny dreams the night before, and she did not report anything unusual. The easy validation I was hoping for eluded me. I had no visible marks on my body, and as the day wore on I began to remember the experience more as a dream than as an actual event. Today when I think about it, the only thing I remember is a 3-second clip of me staring at the closet, believing Ashley is next to me, and the beings are behind me. The rest of the memory is just a recollection of what I wrote down. However, my feeling that they seemed to be taking energy or spirit from me has remained a significant sentiment from that experience.

November of 2009

Several years after Ashley and I separated, I started sensing a heaviness in my home. Something felt off, as if a fountain of negativity was flowing freely within my walls. It brought with it a sense of emptiness and a depressing draw. It seemed to pulsate everywhere, but was heaviest in one specific location. The best way I can describe the sensation is as if there was a polar opposite magnetic force, and the closer I got to it, the stronger it pushed back on me, repelling me, causing a pressure to build in my chest that radiated throughout my body.

Central to my home was a hallway that connected my two bedrooms, office, and main bathroom to the rest of the house. My bedroom was at the far end, and I noticed the energy felt heaviest just beyond my bedroom door. At that specific spot, the energy flowed slower, and seemed to push on me like a thick, consuming tar.

I imagined a negative presence lurking there, or a reservoir of stale energy pooling in a hidden realm. No matter what I tried, I couldn't shake the feeling. I re-did the floors, painted the walls, hung new pictures, and even added a fish tank in the heaviest spot to change the flow of energy after reading a book on Feng Shue. But the heaviness hung like a gelatinous soup in that hallway and I couldn't identify the source or remedy for it. One night, however, I stumbled upon something hiding in that hallway, and took my first stand against them.

November 5, 2009

I had a very realistic dream. In my dream, I awoke from my sleep and got out of bed. As I entered my hallway, a dark brown bulbous shape came quickly scurrying towards my feet. It was the size of a small, 10-pound dog but as it came upon me I realized it was no dog at all. It's spindly, stick-like legs fluttered across the floor as it scurried in my direction. It had an engorged bulbous body with a disproportionately tiny head. Instinctively, I scooped it up as it got to me and saw I was holding a giant tick, fat with whatever it had been consuming. As I examined this gigantic parasite, I realized that I was in an altered state and this bug was the source of the heaviness in my home. It had been hanging out in my hallway, growing plump with the steady stream of sadness and loneliness I had been excreting. But as I held it in my hands, I suddenly knew that its feeding time was finished. My awareness of it created a defense against its siphoning abilities, and my fear of it immediately dissipated.

I had a feeling that vibrated through my body with a resonance of "it can't hurt me," ringing clearly and confidently. The bug sensed my awareness and newfound power and began manipulating the scene in an attempt to scare me by making the lights in the home blink on and off. Its resistance to my resistance was futile, however, and moments later I was awake in my bed. I sat up and wondered: What if there are spiritual parasites much like the tick that was in my hallway that feed off of negative emotions? What if this dream showed me that one was *living in my hallway?*

Analysis

The next day, my home felt lighter: the heaviness was gone and energy seemed to flow freely through my home. But my mind raced to find meaning and understanding. I envisioned an entire species, hidden from our conscious perception, infesting this entire planet, sucking us dry. The tick in my hallway was huge – the size of a small dog. It was so fat it looked ready to explode. Was it feeding off of my negative energy? Did I have other parasites in my home, or attached to my body, draining me of my own life force?

March 06, 2010

I was up late tonight, watching TV until around 2 a.m. in bed. As I was drifting in and out of sleep, my computer screen turned itself off and cast darkness into the house.

I fell asleep, and had a sequence of several mini-dreams. The dreams were random with regular interruptions of partial consciousness. During these semi-conscious states, I was hearing strange sounds coming from my office. I can't recall exactly what they were, but do remember hearing noises. I was half-awake at one point, and directly in front of me appeared a large cone-shaped head. It was so close that it must have been sitting on the bed with me. It was facing away from me, as I was staring at the back of its peach-colored head with thin, string-like hair. The head was wrinkled and old looking, piercing the darkness in front of me. I was squinting my eyes, trying to see better and fighting to fully wake up. As I did, the head faded to the wall and disappeared. For a moment, some letters appeared and hovered in the air in front of me, but I cannot recall what they were.

I fell asleep again, and felt paralysis trying to set in. The strange noises in my office continued, and I heard heavy breathing at the foot of my bed. I assumed it was my dogs, but couldn't be sure.

Paralysis was setting in but I managed to open my eyes to a squint. To my right I saw what I first thought was my blanket bunched up, but then realized it was something else. Standing eye-level, about 3 feet tall, was a dark blueish-gray head. Things were very blurry, but it had either a long chin or large nose that poked uncomfortably close to my face. It was standing right next to me! Its presence startled me, but for some reason my fear was much more managed than during previous encounters and I felt calm enough to try to communicate. As if sensing my intention, it started speaking in my right ear. Its voice was sharp and piercing, with a high and squeaky tone, reminding me of the voice from a childhood cartoon I used to watch. I don't know what it said, but it pierced the silence, stating incomprehensible gibberish. I tried to get a better look at it, and my head was pushed forcefully to the left by an unseen presence. Something then aggressively shook my head left and right about three to four times before I gained control of myself. I recaptured movement, but still felt my body being pulled back into the dream-like state of paralysis, as if a connection was still present. My ears were ringing and pulsing in harmony with my heartbeat.

Analysis

During my moments of wakefulness, I felt as if I was not alone – like something, or several things, were all around me, hiding just beyond my perception.

As I battled to maintain control of my awareness and physical body, I sensed they were trying to manipulate my state of awareness, but could only do so while I was falling asleep.

This creature was talking to me but as I tried to gain more control of myself, it shook my head and woke me up. What was it trying to tell me? Did it wake me up because it was afraid of me?

The closest comparison I have to this being would be of a face baring resemblance to the old plague masks with the long, pointed noses. The creature felt menacing in an obnoxious sort of way but more annoying than scary. Although there was an element of fear connected to this encounter, it waned in comparison to previous encounters. I don't know if it was this being or something else that forced my head forward, but whatever did so used a significant amount of force.

June 07, 2010

I was having a dream that I was wandering a loud nightclub. There was techno music blasting and the air was charged with tension, on the verge of conflict. As I scanned the room, my awareness suddenly shifted.

I started feeling as if I was being controlled by something beyond myself and had glimpses, as if out of my body, of my bedroom. I was hearing an obnoxious noise that sounded like the intentional high-pitch singing of a young child. It seemed playful, yet had an energy and tone that seemed to induce a state of fear in me.

My awareness shifted, and I found myself in my bed, lying on my stomach and propped up on my elbows. I sensed something standing outside my bedroom window, but couldn't see what it was. I looked beneath me and saw a tiny, dark-brown creature, singing the obnoxious children's song. It was goblin-like, and seemed to find humor in its song and actions. Its face felt similar to the long-nosed creature from before, and its voice was of a similar pitch.

This little goblin was attached to my chest, sucking something me from like an infant suckles its mother. I felt energy being pulled from my heart and as I realized what was happening, I became locked in a state of paralysis. I fought to stay aware and was able to break free from this state and force myself awake. I sat up in bed, alone in my room, left wondering what I had just encountered, the obnoxious song echoing in my head...

Analysis

What's interesting about this experience is the dream-state I was in prior to becoming aware of the goblin-creature. I was in a nightclub and experiencing growing fear and anxiety. In waking life, such a scene often brought on a state of anxiety in me due to the PTSD I was coping with at the time. The experience left me wondering if this creature induced a specific dream-state to elicit a particular emotional response because the energetic output of that emotion was desirable to the suckling little incubus.

July 5, 2010

At approximately 4:00 in the afternoon, I laid on the couch to watch TV. I was drifting in and *out of sleep, but could hear the TV in the background. I closed my eyes, and from behind me, I heard the obnoxious singing of the goblin-creature. It sounded as if he was walking casually through my kitchen toward me. The singing grew louder, and I sensed it had stopped behind me and was standing directly above my head. It touched me with something; possibly a rod or cane, and I felt electric pain surge through my entire body in waves from the top of my head down through my feet. It really hurt as it pulsed through me with such intense vibrations.*

I was able to remain calm, and immediately told him I was not afraid. I instantly regained control of my body and sat up, confused. The TV was still playing and I was alone in my home, save for my two dogs.

What scared me was how casual and nonchalant he was with his singing, and how impersonal the interaction felt. I couldn't shake the mental impression of a young farm boy tending the flock or harvesting his crops. I felt of little value, as if this creature had little care for my level of awareness and was simply there to use his little rod to extract something from me. The sensation of this creature "tending to his crops" resonated strongly with me.

Based on my own analysis of my personal experiences alone, I began to suspect that these creatures viewed me as a food source. The singing farmer's casual attitude and sing-song felt so routine and normal, I couldn't shake the thought that I was nothing but a crop to him. It seemed to be my energy they desired, specifically energy that was produced whenever I felt afraid. Having gone through a terrible break-up and having suffered from PTSD, I had a steady stream of fearful and negative energy emanating from me for quite some time. I believe my encounter with the tick in the hallway also demonstrated another aspect of the parasites – the opportunists who took advantage of my vulnerable state.

I recognize how crazy this concept sounds: that a variety of parasitic organisms exist beyond our perception and are currently harvesting our negative emotions for their own needs. Some of these creatures may be opportunists, but others may be acting as farmers and we the crops, cultivating us to produce the energetic output of fear and sadness. Whenever I express this idea out loud, I question my own sanity, yet I can't deny the realness of my personal experiences.

In reflecting back on my father's death, I find an overwhelming sense of humility of the human spirit. As mighty, intelligent, and dominant we believe ourselves to be, my father's death has shown me how meek, fragile, and insignificant we can also be. There is a vast universe, or possibly a multitude of universes, all around us. To assume we are all that exists, or that we have dominion over all that exists, would be a fatal mistake based on the short-sighted ignorance of our collective ego! I often fear that my peers will dismiss my suggestion that I've been plagued by energetic parasites throughout my life, but also see no difference in such statements when compared to the initial claims that germs existed within the human body – claims that invisible creatures surrounded us and had the ability to make us ill.

Prior to the invention of the microscope, microorganisms were undiscovered. To claim that there were tiny creatures that lived within the body that possessed the power to make us sick was a laughable statement. That is, until the invention of the microscope and discovery of such creatures. Today, such knowledge is widely accepted science. Creatures invisible to the naked eye do exist, they do infest our bodies, and they do make us ill. With such a concept in mind, is it really that far-fetched to suggest that something exists beyond our physical perception that has the ability to feed off of our energy? Much like a plant absorbs sunlight, why can't we consider these creatures absorb the energy produced through our own biological processes? What I've learned through my research is that I am not alone in my conclusions. These parasites exist around us. They have the power to manipulate our emotions and do so willingly for we are their crop and they our farmers, and it may be time to harvest…

The Predator

In the beginning of this section, I offered several examples of nature consuming itself through the use of parasitism. Organisms infect the minds of their prey, manipulate their thoughts and behavior, and slowly torture them as they consume their energy to sustain themselves. Parasitism is a part of the natural order of life on this planet, and humans are not immune, as has been demonstrated through multiple accounts and studies.

In part 1 of this book, I reviewed mans' connection to the Universe through the electromagnetic field generated by the human heart. This field serves as a transmitter and receiver of data, and may be the extrasensory organ referred to by Strieber's visitor that allows for psychic communication. It may be the mechanism by which remote viewing is possible. Studies have shown that as people interact with one another through this field, they begin to mirror each other's emotions and body language without knowing or understanding the mechanism that influences such harmony between them.

With our awareness of this sensory organ severely diminished, we have little to no consciously-perceivable indication that we may be falling victim to the malevolent manipulation of this field by a crafty and dedicated predator. I believe it is this field that attracted my nighttime visitors. I believe they manipulated this field around me and siphoned it from me in order to satisfy some sort of predatory or parasitic craving. I also believe that these beings were present at the time of my father's death, feeding off of my fear and sadness as I watched him slowly suffer and die. Through my research into this possibility, I have learned I am not alone in my conclusion...

In his final book, *The Active Side of Infinity*, author Carlos Castaneda revealed his most important lesson from his teacher, don Juan Matus. Don Juan was a Yaqui Indian shaman from Mexico who, according to Castaneda, "endeavored for thirteen years to make available to me the cognitive world of the shamans who lived in Mexico and ancient times."[37]

In his series of books, Castaneda detailed the teachings of Don Juan about altered states of consciousness and mans' relationship to the Earth and Universe. He was taught how to prepare magical brews made from various plants and herbs, which would induce shifts in awareness. During his training in altered states of consciousness, Castaneda encountered many beings and creatures that offered teachings, insight, and terror.

In one of his final teachings, don Juan revealed to Castaneda a secret that he referred to as the "topic of topics," discovered by the shamans of ancient Mexico:

"We have a predator that came from the depths of the cosmos and took over the rule of our lives," don Juan explained. "Human beings are its prisoners. The predator is our lord and master. It has rendered us docile, helpless. If we want to protest, it suppresses our protest. If we want to act independently,

---

[37] Castaneda, Carlos (1998) The Active Side of Infinity (pp 219 – 221). New York, NY: Laugan Productions.

it demands that we don't do so..."[37]

He continues:

"...'There is an explanation,' don Juan replied, 'which is the simplest explanation in the world. They took over because we are food for them, and they squeeze us mercilessly because we are their sustenance. Just as we rear chickens in chicken coops, gallineros, the predators rear us in human coops, humaneros. Therefore, their food is always available to them."[37]

Don Juan explained that human beings were encased in a glowing ball of energy that engulfed the body like a cocoon. He referred to this energy surrounding humans as the "glowing coat of awareness." According to don Juan, this energy is what the predators feed off of, and by the time a human reaches adulthood, all that remains of this glowing coat of awareness is a "narrow fringe of energy that goes from the ground to the top of the toes." He explained that the narrow fringe is enough to keep mankind living, but "just barely."[37]

Was this glowing coat of awareness the same as the electromagnetic organ Whitley

Strieber's visitor spoke of? Is it connected to the electromagnetic field produced by the heart as measured in the HeartMath studies? If these predator/parasites are feeding off of our energetic field, does this then limit our ability to connect to the greater universe matrix through this field? How did we fall

victim to such monsters?

The Garden

In exploring the Christian creation myth as recounted in the Book of Genesis, Chapter 1 (Gideons International Version), we are led to believe that an all knowing, all-powerful, and omnibenevolent God created mankind, loves us, but also punished mankind for its sins. According to Genesis, God created heaven and earth along with the waters and beasts, and it was good. Genesis 2 tells us that after creating this world God decided to make man and stated: "Let us make man in our image, after our likeness." God then made man from the soil, and through giving the breath of life through mans nostrils, man became alive with a soul. God then made the Garden of Eden, and placed man in The Garden to care for it. God gave man dominion over the garden and informed man he could freely eat of every tree in the garden, except for the Tree of the Knowledge of Good and Evil. God warned man that if man ate from this tree, he would surely die. God then created animal life in the garden and realized Adam needed help caring for the garden. God placed a deep sleep upon Adam, and removed one of his ribs. From that rib, God made a woman.

The God of Geneses has only one rule: do not eat from The Tree of Knowledge of Good and Evil, for such an act would prove fatal. On its surface, the myth paints a picture that life is good for Adam and Eve. There is no mention of a predator or parasite eating man; there is no mention of any threats to mans' life other than the possibility of death if man consumes the fruit from The Tree of Knowledge of Good and Evil. But the myth comes with some inconsistencies and unanswered questions. For example, why does God refer to himself in the plural when he creates man by stating: "let us make man in our image, after our likeness"? Why does the story imply that God is acting alone if, in fact, he states that he is not?

According to this creation myth as documented in Genesis, man seems to be favored by God. He has been given dominion over the Garden and the Earth, and over the animal life on the planet. However, man has also been charged with caring for the garden. It's not clear in what capacity man's custodial services are required. Genesis explains that Adam names the various life forms in the Garden, but doesn't go into any detail describing his duties beyond that. Genesis tells us that to help Adam in his duties of caring for the Garden, Eve was created from Adam. It goes onto explain that mankind has dominion over everything in the Garden, which may account for society's current belief that man rules the world and is subservient only to God. It may also account for mans' belief that animals are of a lower order than man.

The story of the Garden concludes after Adam and Eve eat from the tree of Knowledge and instead of dying, realize they are naked and feel shame. As punishment, God banishes mankind from The Garden forever, angry that man has become "like God." This story still leaves several questions unanswered. If God was all-powerful, then why couldn't he prevent them from eating the fruit of the tree? If God was all knowing, why didn't God know what they did or were going to do sooner? Is it possible that the story of Genesis is an inaccurate and possibly skewed description that masks a darker agenda?

In exploring the Nag Hammadi Library we find a variant text that expands the creation myth of Genesis and may answer some of the above questions. Contained within Gnostic texts of The Nag Hammadi Library is a book called the *Hypostasis of the Archons*, which explains that the universe was created not by God, but by the Aeon Sophia. As Sophia moved away from the Pleroma, she moved towards the darkness of swirling chaos. When Sophia began her creation, she did so without her male counterpart and therefore created with an imbalance. As she created, the swirling chaos around her infiltrated her creation in what is referred to as the Demiurge. This Demiurge, the first Archon or ruler, was given authority over the creation of the material world by Sophia. Its name was Yaldabaoth. According to the text, this archon was an androgynous being that was lion-like in appearance. It lacked the ability to perceive the divine, and so believed himself to be the only god, stating: "I am God, and there is no other but me."[38]

Yaldabaoth separated the waters from dry land, and he created heaven and earth, much like the God of Genesis. He also created other archons, and together they decided to make man, stating: "(c)ome, let's create a human of soil from the earth." Yaldabaoth, also referred to as Samael, which means ignorant god, blew into the human's face, giving it a soul, which also bares a similar resemblance to the God of Genesis's actions. But the human made by the archons did not get up from the ground for several days. Eventually, Spirit came to the man and entered him, making him a living soul. This man was called Adam.[38]

The archons placed Adam in the garden to watch over and cultivate it. Adam was told that he could eat from every tree in the garden, except from the Tree of Knowledge of Good and Evil. The archons threatened Adam, telling him that if he even touched that tree, he would die.[38]

They then placed a deep sleep upon Adam,

---

[38] Meyer, Marvin (2007) The Nag Hammadi Scriptures. *The Nature of the Rulers* (pp 187 – 198)

and put him in a state of ignorance. While sleeping, they cut him open and removed not a rib, but the spirit of woman from his side. Later in the garden, upon seeing this spiritual woman with Adam, the archons lusted after her and chased after her. The archons caught her, but she laughed as she turned into a tree. She left behind a shadow that resembled herself, and the archons sexually defiled it.[38] The Genesis version of this story leaves out the spiritual aspect of Eve and omits the group of archons lusting after her. Furthermore, Genesis states that Eve was made from Adam's rib, where the Gnostic version tells us that the feminine spirit of Eve was taken or separated from Adam, implying Adam originally was a complete being with both male and female spiritual aspects.

The Gnostic version of the creation myth seems to fill in some of the gaps left open in the Genesis version. We are told that Yaldabaoth believes he is God. He is responsible for creating Heaven and Earth, but we also learn that Yaldabaoth is not the most powerful being, but a byproduct of Aeon Sophia's desire to create. Furthermore, this story tells us that Yaldabaoth/God created other archons and was not alone when he chose to make man. Could this account for God's statement in Genesis of "let us make man in our image?" The archons still grant Adam dominion over the garden with the task of cultivating it. They separate the spirit of woman from man, but then attempt to sexually defile her.

In returning to Genesis, the story continues in the garden where one day, a serpent approached the woman and asked her to eat of the Fruit of the Tree of Knowledge of Good and Evil. The woman reminded the serpent that God had instructed them not to eat from that tree, or even touch it, for they would surely die if they did.

The serpent then tempted the woman, and told her "for God doth know that in the day ye eat thereof, then your eyes shall be opened, and ye shall be as gods, knowing good and evil.

The woman then ate the fruit of the Tree of Knowledge of Good and Evil, and gave fruit to Adam, and he ate as well.

"And the eyes of them both were opened, and they knew that they were naked..." (Genesis 3:7)

Adam and Eve did not die after eating of this tree. Actually, after he learned they had eaten from the tree, God stated: "Behold, the man is become as one of us, to know good and evil...," acknowledging that God is not alone and that Adam and Eve have achieved a similar status to God. What, then, does this tell us about the serpent and about God? At a minimum, we can discern that the serpent was being truthful in its statements to Eve that she would become like God. Since Eve survived the consumption, we also learn that God had been deceptive in his warning not to eat from the tree or they would surely die. Furthermore, after God realized they had become one of "them," he cast Adam and Eve out of the Garden. Why?

According to the Gnostic texts, the female spirit later returned to Adam, taking on the form of the serpent, also referred to as "the instructor." The instructor asked Adam and Eve (of the flesh) about the archon's directions to stay away from the Tree of Knowledge. When Eve told the serpent that touching the tree would cause them to die, the serpent explained that the archons were jealous of the humans, and that if they ate from the tree, Adam and Eve's eyes would be opened and they would see that they were like gods, knowing good and evil. They certainly would not die. The spirit then left from the serpent, leaving it on the earth.[38]

Eve ate from the tree, and gave Adam fruit as well, and he ate. "Their imperfections became apparent in their ignorance. They recognized that they were stripped of the spiritual, and they took fig leaves and tied them around their naked bodies."[38] By eating of the fruit, Adam and Eve came to understand the Archons had kept them in a state of ignorance – that the archons were not their benevolent creators, but rather their jealous owners and slave masters. The fruit, it seems, contained within it some sort of knowledge that lifted the veil of ignorance from anyone who consumed it.

At realizing that Adam and Eve had eaten from the tree, the archons cast them out of the garden. The archons put humanity "into a great confusion and a life of toil, so that their people might be preoccupied with things of the world and not have time to be occupied by the Holy Spirit."[38] Ultimately, the archons brought chaos into the world of men to distract mankind from matters of the spirit. They once again manipulated mans' perception to keep him ignorant on spiritual matters. Why?

What the Gnostics are telling us in this text is that the being we have come to know as God through Genesis is far from a loving, benevolent being who cares for humanity, but rather a group of ignorant androgynous archons set on repressing mankind and our connection to the Holy Spirit. They tried to scare man away from enlightenment by threatening death, and when their plan failed, they cast man out of the garden to be left in a state of total confusion. They specifically state the purpose of placing man in a state of confusion is to hinder mans' connection to the Holy Spirit. We must remember the testimony in Castenada's book that mankind is a prisoner to a predator that keeps man docile and helpless. This predator rears man the way man rears chickens because man serves as a food source for this predator. Is it possible that the God of Genesis is-in-fact a predator, rearing mankind in a "garden" in order to harvest a form of energy connected to the Holy Spirit? Is it possible that the Holy Spirit is synonymous with Castenada's glowing coat of awareness or Strieber's Visitor's electromagnetic organ?

If we look to the Babylonian creation myth known as the Enuma Elish, we see that Marduk, after defeating the goddess Tiamat, commanded Ea to create man "on whom the toil of the gods will be laid so they may rest," (Tablet VI line 8) ultimately creating man into a life of servitude to the gods in assisting them with their tasks. Similarly, the Mayan Popol Vuh creation myth talks of the gods creating man, as it states:

"Let us make him who shall nourish and sustain us! What shall we do to be invoked, in order to be remembered on earth? We have already tried with our first creations, our first creatures; but we could not make them praise and venerate us. So, then, let us try to make obedient, respectful beings who will nourish and sustain us."[39]

These historical creation myths all point to

---

[39] Goetz, D, Morley, S.G. (translated) Popul Vuh. Retrieved from https://archive.org/stream/PopolVuh/1019117-The-Popol-Vuh-English_djvu.txt

gods that view man as a commodity – a *servant* and a *source of nourishment*! In trying to evaluate the validity of this possibility, we can examine our current existence. Would a loving, caring God create a world with so much suffering? One can argue man has free-will and has created it himself. But would a loving God create a world based on the consumption of life for survival? Would a loving, all-powerful God allow for the creation of parasitic life forms that have the power to eliminate the free-will of another in order to slowly consume them in a painfully torturous manner? We can argue that an evil force, sometimes referred to as the Devil or Satan, is to blame for these things. But would an all-powerful God allow such attacks on his creation? Or, can we consider the possibility that life on this planet was designed, or manipulated, to generate a source of nourishment for the gods that is directly connected to the suffering of life and the energetic output produced through suffering? We must ask ourselves, is it possible that the God of Genesis is a gross and intentional misrepresentation of a master of deception – an evil and cunning predator who works to keep mankind in a state of ignorance so man never realizes his true potential through his connection to the universe? If this holds true, then we may understand the true reason why the Gnostics felt the need to hide the texts in the Nag Hammadi Library. Possession of this knowledge could prove dangerous for a predator dependent on the ignorance of its crop in order to sustain and harvest a sufficient amount of nourishment. This could also serve as the reason why so many Gnostics were systematically murdered during the time when the new-testament was being compiled.

Another Glimpse of the Garden

In his book, *Far Journeys*, Robert Monroe details some of his experiences and research into out of body states. Similar to the journey of Zostrianos, Monroe tells a fantastic story of his nightly trips beyond his body to explore a vast universe filled with seemingly unlimited possibility. In addition, he provides a strong background to the research behind his exploration in out of body states through his work at The Monroe Institute.

During his out of body travels, Monroe would often receive information from the intelligent energies he'd encounter in the form of "Related Organized Thought Energy transferred from one soul to another," or "ROTE." Monroe also referred to this information transfer as "thought balls." In his explanation, a ROTE would simply be floated in his direction and he would absorb the ball, which acted as a download of the information he was receiving.

While outside the body, when he'd encounter other consciousness, they'd often float a thought ball to him so he could absorb or download some information in order to understand a particular idea or concept. Once he'd open the energy, he'd frequently find himself fully immersed in a virtual-reality simulation to experience what he was learning directly.

On his journeys, Monroe regularly encountered other forms of consciousness. One of these forms was a regular visitor for Monroe, and he referred to him as "BB." During one of their meetings, BB provided Monroe with a rote that presented a terrifying possibility.

The rote contained information about Earth, humanity, its inception, and purpose. Upon opening the rote, Monroe experienced a creation story that bore similarities to the creation story of Genesis, with certain added and much darker details. The story starts by identifying an important substance, referred to as Loosh, which was described as a desirable form of energy throughout the universe. Monroe explained it as a rare, but necessary commodity.[40]

A being wanted to find a way to produce Loosh artificially, and so it created a garden. Loosh, Monroe explains, "was found to originate from a series of vibrational actions in the carbon-oxygen cycle and the residue was Loosh in varying degrees of purity." In other words, Loosh is an energetic output based on specific emotions created by carbon-based life forms.[40]

The gardener created several crops with varying levels of success in Loosh production. The first crop created by this being resembled early ocean life. It produced Loosh, but of a lower grade and in small quantities. The Loosh from this crop could only be harvested at the moment of death, and "not one moment before." [40]

The second crop was plant based and lived on the surface. The production of Loosh from the second crop was still limited and of a poor quality.[40]

On the third attempt, the crop was much larger and had the ability to move about the garden. They were referred to as the "Mobiles," and upon termination of their life

---

[40] Monroe (1994) Far Journeys (pp 157 – 172)

spans, large quantities of Loosh were produced.[40]

The Mobiles had a very long lifespan and as a result, they almost completely decimated the second crop, which they consumed as nourishment. The Mobiles consumed so much of the second crop, that they almost drove themselves and the second crop into extinction.[40]

According to Monroe, it was at this time that the creator observed something interesting. As the second crop grew scarce, Mobiles would begin to physically fight over the remaining food source. During these battles, the creator observed the Mobiles produced massive amounts of Loosh of a much higher quality. Through this observation, the creator realized that conflict was the catalyst for increased Loosh production and quality. If Loosh production was the purpose for life, conflict was the means of obtaining it. [40]

The creator designed other Mobiles of varying size and designed them to require the consumption of other Mobile creatures in order to survive. Ultimately, life was created to be sustained by the death of other life in order to produce larger amounts of Loosh.

Monroe explains:

"Thus it was that the Rule of the Prime Catalyst came into being. Conflict among carbon-oxygen cycle units brings forth consistent emanations of Loosh."[40] Life requires death, and the cycle continues…

As the garden evolved, the creator gave the Mobiles varying traits that aided them in either killing their prey or protecting themselves from predation. He notes that many of the traits "served neatly to add to and prolong the conflict periods," in order to produce more Loosh. The more suffering ensued, the more Loosh was generated, so the goal of life was not only death, but to produce suffering during the process of death in order to increase Loosh production and quality.[40] One only has to review the parasites section of this book to see this process in action.

When Man was finally created as the fourth crop, the gardener gave Man a piece of himself to ensure constant mobility. He knew Man would continually search to reunite with the source of the Piece of creation he was given. It generated a spiritual longing within Man to reconnect with the original source, thus leading to an unending inner-conflict that would serve as another constant producer of Loosh.[40]

In order to handle the larger quantities of Loosh, Monroe explains that Special Collectors were established. He doesn't explain what these special collectors were, but tells that their job was to harvest Loosh.[40] Could these special collectors be the parasites I encountered in my home?

"The Collectors periodically harvested segments of the Fourth crop. This was done to ensure adequate chemicals, radiation, and other nourishment for the younger, oncoming units. A secondary purpose was to provide occasional extra amounts of Loosh created by such harvesting."[40]

He continues: "To reap such harvest, the Collectors generated storms of turbulence and turmoil in both the gaseous envelope and the more solid chemical formations that were the base of the garden itself. Such upheavals had the effect of terminating life spans of multitudes of the Fourth Crop as they were crushed under the rolling base formation or smothered under waves from the agitated liquid area."[40]

One can't help but to think of the flood story most commonly told in The Bible and repeated across countless other cultures. In addition, according to the creation myths of the Maya, Aztec, and Hopi, we are in the 4th or 5th worlds meaning civilizations have been destroyed several times on this planet. Were they aware of the thinning of the herd that has taken place since the garden's inception? Were these catastrophes intentionally created in order to produce large quantities of Loosh? Was mankind designed to be periodically led to the slaughter in order to produce Loosh for our hungry farmers?

Today, researchers like Graham Hancock and Michael Cremo have compiled extensive amounts of evidence indicating mankind has been on this planet far longer than we have come to believe. Furthermore, their research suggests that high societies existed, flourished, and were destroyed most recently over 12,000 years ago. Do they represent one of the previous worlds lost? Were they destroyed in order to produce large quantities of Loosh? Is this the real reason why information pointing to our forgotten past is repressed by the establishment?

Returning to the garden, Monroe explains that the Loosh being produced was of an unrefined form. One day, however, the gardener noticed small fragments of purified and distilled Loosh coming from the garden. The gardener searched for the source of the distilled Loosh and found two members of the Fourth Crop fighting to the death. The gardener noted that such battles don't normally produce purified Loosh. Upon further investigation, the gardener noticed one of the Fourth Crop units was fighting to protect its offspring, who were hiding close by, watching the battle unfold. The gardener concluded that the purified Loosh was emanating from the Fourth Crop due to its fear of losing its offspring. [40]

Monroe further explains that the gardener noticed these conflicts could not account for all of the purified Loosh being produced. One day, the gardener came upon one of his creations that had received a piece of the gardener. This unit was all alone, was not in conflict, nor was it hungry. Yet it was producing purified, distilled Loosh. After studying the unit, the gardener realized that this unit was lonely, and loneliness caused the production of purified Loosh. In addition,

Monroe states that the gardener split the unit into halves in order to "engender loneliness as they sought to reunite."[40] This statement also bears a striking similarity to the stories in Genesis and The Nag Hammadi where the Archons removed the female spirit from Adam or made woman from Adam's rib. Could the real reason behind the split be to ensure a state of loneliness in order to guarantee a higher production of Loosh?

Monroe explains that pure, distilled Loosh was created through unfillment, but only if such feelings were pushed at a "vibratory level above the sensory bounds of the environment."[40] If this vibratory level is synonymous with the Holy Spirit, then this may explain why the archons felt it necessary to keep man in a state of chaos and confusion, distracted from matters of the Holy Spirit. Man's lack of awareness of this spiritual aspect would allow the gardeners to siphon away his energy without Man's knowledge of it. This also bears obvious similarities to Castenada's glowing coat of awareness, Backster's Primary Perception, and Strieber's visitor's electromagnetic organ. Such a statement, although horrifyingly depressing, is also one of empowerment. If these feelings need to be pushed to a vibratory level above the sensory bounds of the environment, then what happens if we can push our perceptions to those limits and become aware of those vibrations? Would we then be able to prevent the harvesting of our Loosh?

Monroe concludes his testimony by stating: "From experience, the Collectors have evolved an entire technology with complementary tools for the harvesting of Loosh... The most common have been named love, friendship, family, greed, hate, pain, guilt, disease, pride, ambition, ownership, possession, sacrifice – and on a larger scale, nations, provincialism, wars, famine, religion, machines, freedom, industry, trade, to list a few. Loosh production is higher than ever before..."[40]

With knowledge of this process, I wonder, does it have to be?

Cattle

In Dr. Courtney Brown's book, Cosmic Voyage, Brown offers some interesting data through one of his sessions. As explained in part 1 of this book, Dr. Brown used Scientific

Remote Viewing to obtain his data. In his book, he used this technique to gather information about possible alien interactions with the human race. In a session he titled "Remote-Viewing a UFO Abduction," Dr. Brown explains his findings.

Dr. Brown states that in previous attempts, remote viewers attempting to view an abduction were typically fed a substitute signal that "could only be interpreted symbolically." Other viewers attempting to view the same target would receive a different set of data with varying results.[41]

Of his own session, Dr. Brown explains that "(w)hat resulted was a signal containing symbols that the ETs wanted me to understand. Perhaps they were certain that the abduction itself would be misunderstood, so they substituted symbols that conveyed the purpose or meaning behind the abduction instead."[41] Prior to the session, the only thing Dr. Brown knew of the target was the eight-digit target coordinates.

While viewing the target, Dr. Brown described a fenced-in dirt area. Within the

---

[41] Brown (1996) Cosmic Voyage (pp 59-62)

fence, Dr. Brown saw animals and people. The people seemed to be doing a job, which involved controlling the animals. He describes the work as intense, like a "bullfight."

In probing the target further, he felt something was being abused. He described bleachers surrounding the area with many spectators. The people were described as common people shouting and laughing, and this event was a form of entertainment for them.

Dr. Brown continues that the animals feel threatened. "It is as if the people are playing or toying with the animals. The animals appear to be panicky." He did feel that the people inside the fence did not wish to harm the animals, but were entertained by them. He stated that these people were attempting to control the animals, "as if to herd them." He described it as a "training camp" where they were "training the animals to do things."[41]

Moving ahead in time, Dr. Brown concludes by stating "the animals are no longer panicky. Indeed, they are getting food and love from the trainers." In his personal analysis of the session, Dr. Brown explains that first, someone does not want humans to have direct access to this information, which is why the substitute signal was offered. Secondly, he felt that the animals represented humans and the people represented ETs who were training the humans for an unknown purpose. As for the people in the bleachers, he felt they may have been galactic spectators.[41]

Could it be that the animals represented humans, the people were the Collectors Monroe described, and the spectators were the consumers of Loosh throughout the universe? A bullfight would certainly generate the emotions noted as being beneficial for creating Loosh, and when reflecting on the current activities on Earth, one can make an easy comparison.

It's interesting that Dr. Brown mentioned that the people did not want to harm the animals. I would suspect that harming the animals would damage the crop. A farmer can still love his animals, care for them when they are sick, and make them feel safe as he waits for the right moment to slaughter or harvest them. As for the training, were the animals being trained to produce Loosh? Does a farmer not train cattle to move from one location to another? To stand in place when being milked or walk calmly in line while being led to slaughter?

When he looked forward in time, Dr. Brown explained that the animals were no longer panicky, and were receiving food and love. This statement alone does not discount the possibility that the animals weren't still being harvested in some way.

Similarly, at the conclusion of Monroe's book, he described the distant future where humans were no longer panicky but were still able to produce Loosh and did so willingly. Were Dr. Brown and Monroe both reporting on the same subject? Is mankind being tamed to willingly produce Loosh for the farmers?

Gods Plan

As a child, I grew up believing that everything was a part of Gods plan, and not matter how bad something was, there was a benevolent reason beyond my understanding for suffering and hardship. I accepted the condition of the world on faith. I accepted that my loving God had a reason for the suffering of children and the millions of deaths from wars fought in his name. I accepted that this all-powerful *God* chose not to use his power to intervene because such an intervention would violate our free will, even if the execution of our free will violated the freedoms of billions of life forms on this planet. But I have seen too much to accept this fantasy any more. Maybe God's plan simply is to allow for or manifest the suffering of his creation.

Given our scientific, data-driven, evidence-based mindset, one can easily argue that the testimonies referenced in this section, ranging from my experiences, to the biblical accounts, to the testimonies of Monroe and Dr. Brown, are merely speculative interpretations or conjured metaphorical stories. It's important to note, however, that millions of people on this planet accept the biblical testimonies as truth. They believe the accounts portrayed in the Bible as actually having happened. Their belief certainly does not equate validation, but demonstrates a willingness to accept the testimony of persons claiming to have had a mystical experience as evidence. If the testimonies in the Bible are accepted as evidence, then we must consider the modern-day-testimonies by Bob Monroe, Dr. Courtney Brown, Carlos Castenada, Whitley Strieber, and the multitude of experiencers like me with equal evidentiary value, for there does not seem to be a discernible difference, save for time period and the vocabulary utilized to explain an experience, between the biblical testimonies and the modern-day accounts. As we dive deeper into the realms of the paranormal, supernatural, and mystical, we can find a wealth of testimony by a multitude of witnesses claiming similar encounters. Such experiences, it seems, have been going on throughout recorded human history…

Suffering for God

The world is filled with senseless suffering. Animals are tortured daily for food and experiments, forests are being destroyed at an alarming rate, children are starving, and wars are constantly looming. The corrupt are in power, and the benevolent, "God-fearing" people are suffering. Is this the creation of a loving god? Monroe, it seems, has a testimony that better fits our current reality: The Farmer created the world to produce Loosh through suffering. The Farmer designed life to require the death of other life in order to survive.

What must go through an animal's mind as a predator sinks its teeth deep into its flesh? Do they have faith that their death will serve a greater good because it is a part of God's plan? If God is so powerful, then why didn't he design a world where we didn't have to eat each other to survive? The very construct of life itself should give us an indication about the intentions of its design. Yet we continue to turn a blind eye to such a possibility.

If God exists as per the Bible, and he really does love us, then why did he create such a design? The accounts above suggest that God created mankind for a life of servitude to provide nourishment through suffering. If this holds true, then the being commonly referred to as God may actually be something quite different. But what, then, is God? If we define God as omniscient, omnipotent, and omnibenevolent, then why would such a being allow for the suffering of its creation? Why would such a being allow for the Archons to disconnect us from the Holy Spirit? Is there something to be gained through such intense suffering?

If suffering and hardship forces us to evolve, then maybe that is the greater purpose. Maybe this world forces us to rise above the senseless suffering and find a better way. But in order to do so, we first need to recognize our own culpability in this plan. God may have created the world, but we are the active participants in this world. God can continually fix things for us, or he can give us opportunities to fix them ourselves. In doing so we'd become invested. We'd become empowered. We'd become compassionate and caring. If such a scenario holds true, then God must expect Man to question God's motives and challenge his authority, as I've done repeatedly in this book. He may even expect Man to hate him upon Man's realization that the design is terribly flawed and God has failed to prevent the suffering of our loved ones. Such a difficult lesson, then, may actually be one founded on love - a love so great that it will knowingly produce a hatred for the designer in order to empower the participants. But in order for this powerful lesson to be actualized, we need to take action. We need to stand on our own and accept responsibility for what we have been given. And we need to make it better. The challenges and design may or may not be God's intention. But the outcome of such challenges is our responsibility. For if we choose to ignore this possibility and continue to wait for God to save our species, we may find we are fighting an impossible battle that could condemn all of mankind to an eternity of suffering in this life and beyond. We may come to realize that we are no different than the chickens in countless coops around the world. If, however, we can connect to God through the Holy Spirit, then maybe we can evolve beyond the suffering and create a world free from the chaos and turmoil that surrounds us.

In order to do so, we may be forced to redefine our understanding of what God actually is. We may need to make a distinction between creator and creative force. If God is a being that created mankind to produce Loosh, then we may choose to define God not as an all-knowing, all good, and all powerful being, but as an advanced being, directly responsible for the creation of us for selfish purposes (from our perspective), not much different from a scientist in a laboratory breeding rats for experimental research. Such research may produce results that save human lives, but what must that look like from the rats' perspective?

If God is the equivalent to a scientist in a lab, then God would not be the ultimate power or authority, but a part of a greater system. The source of divine power may be the force behind the creation of life that works through God to bring about man's existence. If this holds true, then God must also be on its own journey of growth and learning, and we are a part of its experience much like the lab rat is a part of ours. There should then be a distinction between God – the creator, and God the force, which may very well be what is known as the Holy Spirit. It is this Holy Spirit that connects us to everything. It is this Holy Spirit that may represent the "glowing coat of awareness," the electromagnetic organ, Primary Perception, or the electromagnetic heart field. It is this Holy Spirit that may be our doorway to liberation, if only we could open ourselves to access it.

A Silent Witness

I am not a scientist, and I am not an objective, independent observer. I am a witness, a victim, and a part of this experience. I am, however, also an investigator – trained to follow leads and collect evidence, which is what I have been doing for the last 20+ years. My method of research and exploration on this subject has been based on experience first, followed by my own analysis of the situation, followed by research. Every step of this process has been guided by intuition. Had I done the research first, and then had an experience, I would suspect that the research influenced either my imagination or my perception of an event. That wasn't the case, however. I had the experience first, drew my own conclusions, and then came to find the accounts and research of others telling almost identical stories with similar conclusions. That has to mean something. Multiple accounts just like mine are occurring all over the globe and across the span of time. It has shown me that I am not alone. What surprised me the most, however, was to learn that my father, someone I had assumed was our biggest skeptic, had been having experiences of his own.

He never made any of us feel uncomfortable about anything we did or took an interest in. He'd sometimes joke about my mom's TV choices and sarcastically tell us how much he loved watching "The Mating Habits of Ants," on the Discovery Channel with Mom, but he never put her or my brother and I down for our interests in obscure things.

As we grew older, we took a strong interest in esoteric teachings. My mom even registered her and me for a psychic development course and for about 2 months we would go to class once per week and come home talking about the interesting things we learned. I remember one night we raced home and opened our wallets to the full moon while chanting "Moon, Moon, beautiful Moon: Filler up, Filler up, Filler up!" in hopes of receiving financial good fortune from the moon.

"This is going to make us rich," I told my dad.

"Okay," he responded as he nodded his head approvingly. "I want a new car," he joked.

My dad would simply listen to our stories, make an occasional joke, and smile. He never judged us, and I always felt like he respected our inquiries even if he didn't believe in them. He never spoke about any of the encounters my mom, brother, and I seemed to be having. He didn't seem interested in discussing those things and would usually redirect a conversation if we tried to include him in a discussion. I sometimes wondered if he thought we were insane but loved us too much to ever say anything. One thing was certain: my dad was not having the same experiences as the rest of us when we would brave sleep each night.

One day, however, when I was about 16 years old, I made mention of our encounters to my dad. I may have been talking about a TV program and how scary it was. I expected him to be non-committal in his response and change the subject. Instead, he said something that surprised me.

"I know some nights I wake up and I can't move," he explained as he pinned his arms to his side and tightened his lips demonstrating the paralysis. "I try to scream for them to get away from Mom, but nothing comes out," he continued.

I was shocked. My dad had never made mention of this topic to me and I always assumed it was because he didn't believe it was possible. After hearing his brief description of our now common experience, I began to wonder if his silence served as a means of protecting my brother and me. It allowed us to believe that we may be imagining it. It gave me hope that what was happening was in my head, and at the time it was a welcomed reprieve from a situation that often left me feeling victimized, powerless, and insane.

For the next 17 years, my father never shared another experience with me, and my family and I wonder if he even had any more. Approximately a year before his passing, however, he began telling us about his dreams…

Dreams

On April 16th, 2012, I had a terrifying dream, which I titled: "Invasion Dream," in my journal:

Jenny and I were in the home I grew up in. An invasion began from above. Strange craft were landing and kidnapping people by sucking them inside. The doors would open and pull people close to them and just suck them in. The ships were the size of houses. A large being entered our home. We were in the basement. I think the being was humanoid. I felt powerless and afraid to fight because I could not win. The being killed my pet rat and pet rabbit with a needle and they died at my feet. He then injected my dogs, Gizzmoe and Buddy, with sliver needles filled with green ooze. I couldn't save them and they died at my feet and in my arms. They oozed green and their bodies compressed. I felt they were killed to show I had NO control and we were powerless to stop this from happening.

The being was trying to change us, to make us more like him. I wanted to resist so I threw a knife and stabbed it in the chest. Its body wiggled like rubbery jelly as it smiled and pulled the knife out. I couldn't hurt it. It threw me around forcefully. I was so helpless.

The creature then put green sludge in my ear. I knew it was going to change me. I felt my body would become rubbery like the beings, so when it looked away I removed the sludge. I think Jenny was being changed as well, but I couldn't see her.

I was assigned jobs to do in our basement. I felt enslaved and feared being killed. I was over the sink & hanging a drop ceiling. I was trying to do something with PVC pipe over the faucet to the ceiling, but I needed to keep it hidden. I don't understand why, but it was an act of defiance. I wasn't working fast enough & it called me outside.

The being had taken on the appearance of my father. My mom and brother were there – and I still had a strong feeling of a total loss of control. It began acting as if it was teaching us things - but I still felt like it owned me. The creature that now looked like my father tried to sound friendly and I told him he couldn't control everything. I told the creature it couldn't control me if I took my own life. I was so afraid and did not want to live in a world of such slavery and control. . . "

I didn't share this dream with anyone. I recorded it in my journal and kept it to myself. But it was a terrifying experience. As I'm incorporating my dream into this book, I'm finding strong metaphors hidden within this experience. The sense of being owned, the use of fear for manipulation, and the visions of death of my pets are consistent with the idea that we are being manipulated by an unseen force to promote suffering. It seemed so real, and at looking back, I find it significant that this creature took on the appearance of my father, for just 14 months later he was gone. What was even more surprising, was that my father shared the same dream…

On August 24, 2012, four months after my "Invasion Dream," I received a concerning email from my mother. My father had a terrifying nightmare, and was completely shaken by it. He was so upset he could barely speak. My mom went onto explain that they slept in that morning, but woke up still feeling tired. As soon as they were awake, my dad explained the following dream to her:

All of us were in our old home (the same setting as my "Invasion Dream"). Hundreds of spaceships were beaming down red lights at the Earth as orange disks were being thrown and falling to Earth with a loud bang. Dad met a being eye to eye at our back door (the same door I encountered the being that became my father). Dad slammed and locked the door. He described the being as looking like the "Creature from the Black Lagoon," and kept saying they were here to destroy us.

"We're all fucked," he kept saying. "We're fucked."

My mom also recalled glimpses of her dream from the previous evening. She encountered a being dressed in black wearing a black mask.

She could only see its eyes, and when she touched it she felt something was wrong.

As the two discussed their dreams and feelings, they noticed (in waking reality) what my mom initially described as bubbles rising up from the front yard. They ran outside and found a swarm of termites emerging in a beautiful display of ascension from an old oak tree.

"It was so beautiful, as the sun was radiating brilliantly behind them, giving them a divine glow as they rose up toward the sky," she explained.

The timing of their emergence was interesting, as these elegant parasites had finished their consumption of their host, the mighty Oak - the king of the forest - and began their ascension into the light. In looking back on the entire scenario, I have to wonder if the dreams shared by my father and I represented the attack on his body, and the parasites that consumed him, the mighty Oak of our family, were much like the termites, draining the life from their host until it was time for them to move out into the world to infect and consume their next victims.

I also wonder if my father and I both viewed an

alternate timeline where an event like this actually happened. I don't know why we'd both be shown the same event, but because of the power of my experience and the fact that my father shared such a similar event, it seems incredibly significant and important.

There is a connection through this wireless-psychic-Internet we seem to have access to, and my father and I had tuned into the same frequency. If this dream was somehow a message warning us of my father's coming death, then we may be ignoring access to a tool that could turn the tides in this conflict of victimization by the parasites. We need to pay attention to our dreams and get better at interpreting the signs given to us. Ignoring them, I've learned, can have grave consequences…

Part 3: Manipulation of the Holy Spirit

Energetic Power

Through the work of Clever Backster, we've learned that plants can perceive human intention and the emotional outputs of other organisms with their Primary Perception. Strieber's visitor spoke of an electromagnetic organ just above the skin that allows for psychic communication. The HeartMath Institute measured the electromagnetic signal generated by the heart that is capable of transmitting and receiving emotional data. Carlos Castenada told us of the "glowing coat of awareness." We've learned that psychic communication is possible, and quite common, even if we're not consciously aware of the ongoing exchange between ourselves and our environment. We've been conditioned to tune out these signals, and no longer consciously commune through this network, and therefore have lost touch with the world around us. We've lost touch with ourselves, and as a result forgotten who we truly are. We have become weak and vulnerable to the manipulation of this field that has become a Trojan Horse into our psyche that may be intelligently directed to influence our behaviors, our feelings, and our actions to the will of those in control. But what would happen if we once-again learned to utilize this sense? What would happen if we came to rely on our 6th sense as often as we rely on our sense of sight or smell? As remote viewing research has shown us from the Stanford Research Institute and The Farsight Institute, anybody can learn this technique. According to Strieber's visitor, this sense can be strengthened. And according to Strieber's visitor, we can "haunt God"…

Based on the research and testimony compiled in this book, it would seem that the electromagnetic field surrounding the human body would act as the perfect gateway for these invisible parasites to manipulate human thought and behavior. It is through this field that we are being manipulated to produce suffering, loneliness, and fear. It is through this field that we are controlled. It is through this field, however, that we find liberation for we can use this field to change the negative flow into something positive.

As Fredrich Niche once stated: "Whoever fights monsters should see to it that in the process he does not become a monster. And if you gaze long enough into the abyss, the abyss will gaze back into you." [42]

Presently, many scream for revolution. They take to the streets and proudly shout in support of their cause or in opposition to their oppressors. Although their reasons may be benevolent, their pursuit of change builds tension and conflict. It charges the surrounding energetic atmosphere with stress and negativity, infecting those who come into contact with it, spreading negativity like an airborne virus. Although intentions may initially be noble, the rage of negativity blinds the masses from their benevolent objectives and festers like a plague. Revolutionaries and advocates for change may one day find themselves using the same tactics they are protesting in order to fight the oppressors using such tactics. In essence, they find they

[42] Nietzche, F. (2002) Beyond Good and Evil. (PDF) New York, NY, Cambridge University Press. Retrieved from https://www.holybooks.com/wp-content/uploads/Nietzsche-Beyond-Good-and-Evil.pdf

have become the monsters they are fighting. This could, in part, be connected to the electromagnetic field of emotion. If one was to gaze into this abyss of emotional energy long-enough without grounding themselves in awareness and positive emotion, the abyss of emotion may then gaze into them and affect their thoughts, feelings, and actions while also creating a plethora of Loosh in the process. When advocating for change, we should consider creating the change we want instead of fighting the force of opposition, for as Dr. King stated:

"Darkness cannot drive out darkness; only light can do that. Hate cannot drive out hate; only love can do that. Hate multiplies hate, violence multiplies violence, and toughness multiplies toughness in a descending spiral of destruction… The chain reaction of evil – hate begetting hate, wars producing more wars – must be broken, or we shall be plunged into the dark abyss of annihilation."[43]

In order to bring about peace, we need to become peace. We need not fight evil, for in doing so we run the risk of committing evil acts and becoming evil ourselves. Imagine a

[43] King, M.L. (1963) Strength to Love.

world where each individual town and municipality employed a small population of meditators. Their job would be to focus on peace and cleanse the energetic fields in their given area. As we explored in this chapter, imagine if this technique was taught and practiced in all schools. The positive flow would be overwhelming and may play a major role in the reduction of conflict and suffering. It may eliminate the desire and even the need for protest and instead produce harmony among communities. Violence begets more violence. What can peace produce?

Reiki

About a year after my father died, Jenny, my wife, enrolled me in a Reiki course. She thought it would be good for me since I had expressed a strong interest in "alternative" (traditional) healing methods after his passing. I was having a tough time with life in general, as my worldview had taken a dark turn after his death, and I was consumed with anger and frustration over my newfound perceptions of reality. At that point in my life, I was convinced that we were mere cattle being consumed by energy-hungry monsters, and we were powerless to stop their incessant manipulation and feeding off of us. Jenny hoped Reiki would bring something positive into my life and restore some of my hope and faith in the world. I had no idea what Reiki was, so I did a little reading on the Internet about a week before the course began. It was described as a "Japanese method of relaxation that promotes healing", which didn't make much sense to me. My skepticism was immediately high, and I didn't expect to learn anything of value.

My instructor provided a book for all of the students to read prior to the course, and I navigated the pages with some interest. I learned about the history of Reiki in Japan, and how it helped many people after the atomic bombs fell. I read about the many success stories found through Reiki, and I studied the process of delivery. I looked at hand positions, breathing, and read about the Reiki attunement we would receive during our training, which would unlock our bodies to allow Reiki energy to flow through us. At this point, I was starting to suspect the design of this healing system was a business model, and didn't have much faith in coming away from the course with any real healing ability, despite all the testimony in the book.

During training, however, my perspective gradually began to change. Our instructor gave us an attunement by standing behind each one of us, drawing Reiki symbols over our heads, and bestowing Reiki energy on us. We were then paired off to practice Reiki on one-another and, still skeptical, I noted that I didn't feel any different or more gifted than I had prior to the attunement. The instructor explained that some of us might experience an increase in psychic abilities, especially if such abilities had manifested in our lives previously, but that could take a few days to a week to develop. I doubted anything unique would happen to me, but was hoping that I would get to experience something.

My first partner was a woman about my age. She was dressed in sweatpants and a sweatshirt and appeared completely average. Nothing about her physical appearance indicated that she had any ailments or illnesses. She lay on the table with her hands at her sides, and I began practicing the hand positions we were taught by placing both of my hands at the top of her head. I visualized the Reiki energy coming in through the top of my head, entering my heart, and then flowing out through my hands into this woman's body. After about a minute, my hands began to tingle and pulsate. I felt heat coming out of my hands and the woman told me she felt warmth coming from them. I closed my eyes for a few moments and took a deep breath.

When I opened them, floating in front of my face was a tiny pair of transparent purple lungs. They were maybe a foot in front of my face, eye level, and about 6 inches in height. I blinked my eyes, but found they were still there, hovering in front of me. After a moment they faded away into nothingness. I decided to explore the vision I had, but heard the voice of doubt and ridicule screaming at me to keep quiet:

What if I'm wrong?

She's gonna think you're crazy!

It was just your imagination!!!

This isn't possible!

"I know this is going to sound weird," I started, "but I just saw a pair of lungs floating in front of my face. Does that mean anything to you?"

She immediately responded: "Oh my gosh, yes! I have asthma and was sick with bronchitis last week. How did you see that?"

"I'm not sure," I said. "A pair of tiny lungs just appeared in front of me."

Intrigued, I moved onto my next partner. This time I practiced an energy sensing technique where I moved my hand over the top of her body to detect fluctuations in her energy field. I felt a slight tingling sensation over her body as I moved my hands through various regions. When I reached her leg, the tingling sensation grew stronger. I stopped with my hands hovering over her knee where it seemed to be strongest and asked her about it. She explained that she injured her knee and had been experiencing some pain there.

Several of us in class shared similar experiences with the Reiki energy. As we went through the healing process, we gathered impressions about our partners as the energy flowed through us to heal our varying ailments. Although exciting, these psychic experiences were nothing like I was expecting. In my mind, I envisioned my body going into a deep trans state. I expected to convulse heavily and have my eyes roll to the back of my head whenever I'd begin a session, like some Hollywood-possessed shaman. I even half-expected to start speaking in foreign tongues as my body convulsed and levitated, firing beams of blinding white light from my eyes and mouth. Fortunately, the psychic process of

Reiki was nothing like this at all. Besides a slight tingling in my body at times, I felt completely normal. My visions seemed more like tricks of light than elaborate psychic manifestations. In short, there was nothing fantastic about the feelings I experienced as I obtained psychic data. It was quite the opposite, actually, and felt quite casual. These events felt so regular and bland that they could easily have been dismissed as tricks of light, imagination, or a wide array of other excuses.

Prior to the end of class, my instructor shared a personal account with us. He was talking about Reiki energy and said that it was synonymous with what the Chinese call "chi," and what the Yogi's refer to as "prana."

"Reiki is a universal life-fore that exists everywhere," he stated. "When we deliver Reiki, the energy is not coming from us, rather, we are acting as a channel for the Reiki to enter into our bodies and direct itself into whomever we are working with."

He explained that one day while he was practicing Reiki, he heard a voice in his head. The voice told him he needed to teach Reiki. He questioned the origin of the voice and the voice responded that Reiki is the Holy Spirit. I paused for a moment at hearing this, and realized my skepticism went on high alert. The Holy Spirit was a religious term, and I had no interest in religion after giving up my Christian faith years ago. Because of the religious undertones, I immediately wanted to reject everything he was telling me. But I couldn't – not after the sessions I had just experienced: I had the visions during healing sessions and I felt the energy flowing through me as it soothed my classmates injuries. But surely that wasn't an indication that the Holy Spirit was present. Or was it? Did I have to adhere to religious doctrine in order to practice Reiki? Or was religion trying to explain a universal concept as it applied to its religious doctrine?

I reflected on what I knew of the Holy Spirit. Being raised Catholic, the term Holy Spirit was a regular reference throughout the first 20 years of my life. Each day when I'd bless myself, I'd recite: "In the name of the Father, and of the Son, and of the Holy Spirit, Amen." I knew the Father meant God, and the Son meant Jesus, but couldn't really describe the Holy Spirit in words other than

"Holy Spirit." This perplexed me. What was the Holy Spirit? Why was it important in the Catholic faith? As I explored this thought and compared it to the Reiki process, I realized that Catholic's bless themselves by touching their forehead first, then down to their heart, to the left shoulder, and then the right shoulder before stating: "Amen" while bringing hands together in prayer in front of the heart. This, I was told, symbolizes the sign of the Christian cross. In Reiki, I was taught (and later actually felt) that Reiki energy comes into the crown of the head, travels to the heart, and then moves out to the hands where it is released to the person receiving the healing. To begin a Reiki session, practitioners first cleanse their energy by rubbing the left arm, then the right, and then bring the hands together in front of the heart. The Catholic blessing in the sign of the cross moves in exactly the same way Reiki energy flows through the body. I suspect the Christian doctrine understood the power of this energy at one point, but most likely lost the understanding of it as doctrine was established and the connection was lost.

Regardless of religious beliefs and doctrinal terminology, I have experienced undeniable results through the use of Reiki. It has given me access to information I'd otherwise have no way of knowing. One afternoon I gave Reiki to a woman, and while going through the session, I closed my eyes only to find a man staring back at me from behind my eyelids. I opened my eyes and then closed them again, and the man was still there. During the session, I sensed the woman was experiencing a lot of stress, which was manifesting in some stomach problems she was having. The woman confirmed my perceptions, and I continued with the session. When I finished, I told her about the face that was staring at me. I described the man's brown hair, approximate age (20s) and shabby beard. I expected her to tell me she wasn't sure who he was, or to take a while and try to think of someone who fit that description. Instead, she immediately told me: "That's my son. He is the reason I am having so much stress. We have been in conflict for a while now." I was shocked, because I had no way of knowing who her son was and what he looked like, and certainly had no way of knowing that he was the cause of the stress I had perceived. But it all connected.

Through other sessions, I've been able to pinpoint troublesome areas and offer healing and comfort to people in distress. Sometimes a part of their body will start glowing in a bright color, and although I'm still not sure what different colors mean, I recognize that these areas are in need of my attention. By telling my clients what I am seeing, they often validate that there is in-fact something going on in that specific area.

One morning, I was sitting in my bedroom talking with Jenny when I noticed a pink glow appear around her stomach. I tried to ignore the glow, but no matter what I did, it wouldn't go away. It became a distraction to our conversation, as I kept focusing on her stomach instead of her eyes while she was talking. Finally, I interrupted her sentence:

"Is there any chance you're pregnant?" I asked.

She froze. "Um… No? Why did you just ask that?"

"I see a pink light coming from your belly, and I'm not sure what it means."

"There is no way I can be pregnant," she explained. "I'm not even due to have my period for another week."

"Okay. It's probably just my eyes acting funny," I said, slightly embarrassed.

About a week later, however, Jenny was so freaked out by what I had told her, she decided to take a pregnancy test just to rule out the possibility. To her surprise, the test came back positive! Jenny was pregnant and a little confused at how I was able to determine she was pregnant at a time when home-pregnancy tests would not have been able to detect the pregnancy. I have no idea why I saw that glowing pink aura, and I have no idea how to "turn on" that sense all the time. It sometimes pops up when I'm performing Reiki, and it sometimes pops up in the most random places without any rhyme or reason. Sometimes I wonder if it is the Reiki energy choosing what it wants me to see as opposed to me choosing when to see what I want. Whether it's my direction or Reiki's intention, I am certain that the more I open up to and work with this energy, the more perceptions I have received.

Through Reiki, I have experienced the personal validation I needed to authenticate some of what is discussed in this book. It has allowed me to witness what is possible through our electromagnetic field and shown me that anyone is capable of strengthening this sense. It has also led me to realize that as amazing as a Reiki healing session can be, I have only scratched the surface of what we are all capable of achieving.

The Maharishi Effect

So what can we do with this untapped power of ours? How can it enrich our lives and better the world? What do we need to do to access this force? We can use this sense to offer healing – to ourselves, our community, and to the world, and fortunately, there is compelling research to support that claim.

In the 1970s, research was conducted in an attempt to understand the correlation between people practicing Transcendental Meditation and violence & crime in a particular area. What the studies found was that a small number of meditators have the ability to reduce criminal activity in a targeted area through the practice of Transcendental Meditation.

According to the Transcendental Meditation website, TM.org, Transcendental Meditation is "an effortless technique for 'recharging your mind and body' – and creating a brighter, more positive state of mind." Research has shown that TM reduces stress and anxiety and improves brain function and cardiovascular health.

Studies into the impact of TM on crime, which came to be known as the Maharishi Effect, were conducted in a wide range of locations and all boasted similar results. In 1981, a study was conducted in the US involving multiple cities. The study looked at pairs of cities with populations larger than 10,000. 1 percent of the population in experimental cities had been instructed in the TM technique by the end of 1972. Control cities had a significantly lower population of TM trainees with a mean percentage of .22 percent. The study looked at crime totals for each of the experimental and control cities for each year between 1967 and 1977. The years 1967 to 1972 served as the pre-intervention period, while 1972 – 1977 were the post-intervention period. What the study found was a decrease in the crime rate among the experimental cities. "The decrease was evident both immediately after the cities reached the 1-percent level of TM program participation and in the crime rate trend during the subsequent 5 years. The findings imply that persons taking TM will influence others, including the crime-prone population." Ultimately, Transcendental Meditation seems to have a direct effect on the levels of crime in a given area.[44]

With an understanding of the cardio-electromagnetic communication as explained by HeartMath, it shouldn't come as a surprise that the TM techniques work to reduce violence and crime in a given area because meditators are changing the electromagnetic field that then has a direct impact on anyone interacting with that field. Much like one could change the PH level of a fish tank to affect the behaviors of fish, we can change the PH level of our energetic fish-bowl to positively (or negatively) impact those who swim among us. By simply meditating, we possess the power to increase levels of peace in a given area.

---

[44] Dillbeck, M.C., Landrith, G., Orme-Johnson, D.W. (1981) Transcendental Meditation Program and Crime Rate change in a Sample of Forty-Eight Cities. *Journal of Criminal Justice, Volume 4 (pp 25 – 45)* Retrieved from https://www.ncjrs.gov/App/Publications/abstract.aspx?ID=852 19

Meditation School

In an effort to address an inner-city school systems many academic and behavioral challenges, schools within the city of Baltimore partnered with the Holistic Life Foundation to create school-wide mindfulness programs. These programs involve meditations at the beginning and end of the day, yoga practice, breathing techniques, and access to a mindfulness room for students needing to refocus and center themselves.

According to a study released in 2010 titled "Feasibility and Preliminary Outcomes of a School-Based Mindfulness Intervention for Urban Youth," bringing mindful meditation to the schools in Baltimore has had a positive impact on "problematic responses to stress including rumination, intrusive thoughts, and emotional arousal." According to the study, "findings suggest that a mindfulness-based intervention...shows promise in reducing problematic physiological and cognitive patterns of response to stress among youth."[45]

A 2016 Washington Post article reports that at Robert E. Coleman Elementary in Baltimore, "Students still get sent to the principal – 30 times last year – but not as often as they once did. For the past two years, there have been no suspensions at Coleman."[46]

The article continues to explain that "Patterson Principal Vance Benton said his school practices breathing during a recorded announcement in the morning, similar to Coleman. It also has a Mindful Moment Room…" The article reports that "Suspensions are down at (Patterson) – 22 this school year, compared with 46 last year at the same time."[46] That's just over a 50% reduction in school suspensions.

Many of the students in attendance at these Baltimore schools "see drug dealing and hear

---

[45] Medleson, Tamar, Et al. (May 2010) Feasibility and Preliminary Outcomes of a School-Based Mindfulness Intervention for Urban Youth. *Journal of Abnormal Child Psychology 38*(7):985 – 984. Doi: 10.1007/s10802-010-9418-x

[46] St. George, Donna (2016, November 13) How Mindfulness Practices are Changing an Inner-City School. Retrieved from https://www.washingtonpost.com/local/education/how-mindfulness-practices-are-changing-an-inner-city-school/2016/11/13/7b4a274a-a833-11e6-ba59-a7d93165c6d4_story.html?noredirect=on&utm_term=.62a4ab90bd9a

sirens or gunshots; some don't have stable housing, some worry about relatives getting locked up."[46]

As a former urban educator, I have worked in similar neighborhoods. My students faced a level of crime, violence, and trauma that, in my opinion, resembled that of a war zone. I often wonder what impact the meditation and mindfulness techniques taught in Baltimore schools would have in the schools I've taught in. I wonder what impact mindfulness and meditation would have on the surrounding communities if every school in the city implemented these programs. If my students had learned to stop and breath instead of throwing fists when frustrated, those schools would be significantly less violent.

We live in a world where citizens are now calling for more security, more police, and in some cases, armed teachers in our schools. Such a culture, I fear, only contributes to the electromagnetic signal of fear and aggression that, in turn, will only work to magnify the intensity of an already persistent signal. Through meditation, however, we have the power to stop this infectious signal at its source. We can use that signal to change the energetic influence and ultimately the negative behaviors of a population to promote peace within the community. Doing so may also serve to starve our energetic parasites out of our lives.

The Maharishi Effect has shown us we only need 1% of a given population meditating to impact change. Imagine if every-single-school in the country trained students to meditate. Imagine the world we could create…

Manipulation of Human Behavior

It's no secret that human behavior can be influenced by a variety of factors in our environment. Some are apparent and others are not. The food we eat and drugs we consume can impact our health, our thoughts, and our actions. Certain substances, like the psilocybin magic mushroom, may work to enhance or alter consciousness, and others, like alcohol, to hinder it. Much like the physical substances we ingest into our bodies, there are other non-physical forces that can impact us just as strongly. We can't see radiation, yet it can have a variety of physical impacts on our bodies.

It's unfortunate that the limits of human perception have served as boundaries to our understanding of and relationship to this world. Some of our laws and rules, although utilized to guide and teach us about this existence, have also served to limit what may be possible. If we can't categorize, measure, or experience something, we often assume it must not exist. We are, however, running blindly through this universe, as the five human senses are only capable of sensing a tiny fraction of what is actually out there around us. Who are we to say that just because we cannot see it, hear it, taste it, smell it, or feel it, it must not exist? Germs were an unknown existence until discovered, yet they had (and continue to have) a strong influence over the health and welfare of the human body. Before the microscope, science had no means of measuring their existence – but they were there! Looking back, we could measure their affects based on the symptoms they caused, whether it was fever, rash, nausea, or headache, but failed to identify them as the actual cause of such ailments.

Although we have not (yet) invented the energy parasite "microscope," we may be able to measure the symptoms that correlate with an energetic parasite infestation. Much like physical parasites such as the emerald wasp or Toxoplasma gondii (the cat amoeba) have proven their ability to alter their hosts' behavior negatively, energy parasites may be a contributing factor to depression, suicide, and acts of cruelty. Their influence may be the causing factor behind negative self-talk and decisions that bring harm to life. They may be present and feeding on victims of depression, anxiety, and paranoia. If we can identify these symptoms, we may be able to find a way to address them and eventually treat the cause, cleansing ourselves of these problematic creatures. Presently, we have not created a microscope capable of detecting these parasites. However, research has proven that it is possible to manipulate human behavior and emotions through the same electromagnetic mechanism proposed in this book. This in-it-of-itself does not prove the existence of energy parasites, but does suggest that if they do exist, it would be possible for them to affect the human body through the electromagnetic field.

Patents

On June 1, 2002, Hendricus G. Loos filed U.S. Patent Number 6506148, titled: Nervous System Manipulation by Electromagnetic Fields from Monitors. This patent described a technology that utilizes an electromagnetic field generated through computer monitors and television screens to interface with the naturally-occurring electromagnetic field running through the human body. The abstract to the Patent states the following:

"Physiological effects have been observed in a human subject in response to stimulation of the skin with weak electromagnetic fields that are pulsed with certain frequencies near 1/2 Hz or 2.4 Hz, such as to excite a sensory resonance. Many computer monitors and TV tubes, when displaying pulsed images, emit pulsed electromagnetic fields of sufficient amplitudes to cause such excitation. It is therefore possible to manipulate the nervous system of a subject by pulsing images displayed on a nearby computer monitor or TV set. For the latter, the image pulsing may be imbedded in the program material, or it may be overlaid by modulating a video stream, either as an RF signal or as a video signal. The image displayed on a computer monitor may be pulsed effectively by a simple computer program. For certain monitors, pulsed electromagnetic fields capable of exciting sensory resonances in nearby subjects may be generated even as the displayed images are pulsed with

subliminal intensity."[47]

The patent claims the ability to induce the following effects: "ptosis of the eyelids, relaxation, drowsiness, the feeling of pressure at a centered spot on the lower edge of the brow, seeing moving patterns of dark purple and greenish yellow with the eyes closed, a tonic smile, a tense feeling in the stomach, sudden loose stool, and sexual excitement, depending on the precise frequency used and the skin area to which the field is applied." By simply watching a television program or movie, this technology allows for the manipulation of a multitude of unknowing participants.

On July 21, 1998, Loos obtained U.S. Patent 5,782,874, "Method and apparatus for manipulating nervous system." This patent claimed to work as "an aid to relaxation, sleep, or arousal, and clinically for the control and perhaps the treatment of tremors and seizures, and disorders of the autonomic

---

[47] Loos, H. G. (2001, June 1) Nervous system manipulation by electromagnetic fields from monitors. United States Patent 6,506,148. Retrieved from http://patft.uspto.gov/netacgi/nph-Parser?Sect1=PTO1&Sect2=HITOFF&d=PALL&p=1&u=%2Fne tahtml%2FPTO%2Fsrchnum.htm&r=1&f=G&l=50&s1=6506148 .PN.&OS=PN/6506148&RS=PN/6506148

nervous system, such as panic attacks."[48] Such technology can have tremendous beneficial impacts on patients and demonstrates some of the potential impact possible through the technological manipulation of the electromagnetic field. Ultimately, it again represents an ability to manipulate human mood and behavior by means of the electromagnetic field.

What these two patents demonstrate is the vulnerability of the human central nervous system to influence and manipulation of human behavior via the electromagnetic field. It shows us that our internal software is vulnerable to attack from various forms of malware that are projected in our direction. It also shows that there are developers focused on manipulating humanity through the use of this field. It can easily be embedded in a television show or computer program, therefore unknowingly affecting the behaviors of anyone who is close enough to be impacted. This technology is possibly

---

[48] Loos, H.G. (1998, July 21) Method and apparatus for manipulating nervous system. United States Patent 5,782,874. Retrieved from http://patft.uspto.gov/netacgi/nph-Parser?Sect1=PTO1&Sect2=HITOFF&d=PALL&p=1&u=%2Fne tahtml%2FPTO%2Fsrchnum.htm&r=1&f=G&l=50&s1=6506148 .PN.&OS=PN/6506148&RS=PN/5782874

already in our homes, and quite possibly deployed through our cell phones.

When exploring this vulnerability to manipulation, I can't help but to recall the testimony of Bob Monroe and his data regarding the garden: The design of life to produce Loosh. Could this electromagnetic vulnerability be an intentional design to allow unseen access to the human psyche in order to instill a state of loneliness or suffering to collect Loosh? Or is this aspect of humanity simply being exploited by, as Castenada accounts, a cunning predator? We also must recall the Gnostic teachings, where once mankind realized they were like gods, the Archons cast them from their garden into a life of confusion to distract them from matters of the Holy Spirit. Why?

Our electromagnetic component does seem to be our connection to this matrix reality, and could potentially act as a liberating ability. However, without proper safeguards and awareness of this, our internal software could certainly be compromised and an infectious signal could easily be disseminated across a wide mass of people to manipulate them to desired forms of output. (The fear-based mainstream media comes to mind). The Maharishi Effect has shown us that only one percent of the population is needed to impact the greater community through this field. What percentage of people watch television daily and are possibly receiving these *negative* signals?

In coming back to our germ analogy, without awareness of germs, there was no need to wash hands before performing tasks like eating or surgery, which left people vulnerable to their infestations. However, once we learned of the existence of microorganisms, we were able to put safeguards in place to minimize their impact on human health. In knowing that we are vulnerable to manipulation through the electromagnetic field, should we not be working on safeguards to mitigate the potentially harmful effects as well?

This field exists all around us, and we are all capable of learning to perceive it. With perception of the field, we can also learn to identify changes to it, which may indicate an attempted tampering with our energy. It gives us a first-line-of-defense against possible attacks or predation via technology or energetic parasites. In order to be aware of this field, however, we first must become aware of ourselves. As I mentioned in the very beginning of this book, I sensed an attack on my energy when I encountered the man in the bookstore. My recognition of that attack allowed me to make a choice to leave the area to a point of safety where I was no longer vulnerable to his actions. By becoming aware of our energetic sense, we can recognize when it is being tampered with or influenced. We will then have the ability to make a choice. We can choose to ignore the signal, and allow it to perform whatever task it was assigned, or we can choose to counteract those efforts by either creating a countersignal or removing ourselves from its sphere of influence.

As my father lie dying on his hospital bed, I detected that signal and made the choice not to fight it, but to counter it. I was being flooded with the emotions of fear and sadness, but instead of lashing back defensively with anger, I created the opposing frequency of love in my heart. I thought of the wonderful memories I had with my father – the laughs we shared and the things we'd done – and was able to feel joy and happiness during that difficult time. Although still sad and afraid for my father, I felt my emotional and energetic output change. I felt lighter and empowered in the face of tragedy. It was shortly after I made this switch from fear to love that my father finally passed. To this day I don't know if my shift had anything to do with his release, but I often hope it brought him comfort.

Strieber's visitor told us we can improve on our electromagnetic sense. Remote viewing practices and research have proved this is a true statement. But we have to make a choice. We first need to choose awareness of this sense. We then need to choose to listen to it. Doing so could lead to our greatest acts of liberation and offer protection from harmful signals, whether coming from the technology of our electronic devices or the ill-intended actions of our invisible energetic parasites.

Purpose

At times it seems like our existence is engulfed in a continual state of suffering. Perpetual wars, famine, disease, hunger, homelessness, and horrible acts of animal cruelty proliferate the entire planet. When we find ourselves caught in the middle of one of life's many hardships, we may wonder about the reason for such suffering, but more often than not are quick to rationalize the problem with trite little sayings such as: "it's God's will," or "Everything happens for a reason." With such a statement, we are then able to continue on with our lives, believing we are powerless to enact change to prevent future suffering for ourselves or anyone else in the world because a higher power wills it to be so. In other words, such sayings empower us to do nothing.

But why? Why do we continually allow for suffering of life on this planet? Does our species as a whole crave the suffering of our fellow man and animal life? Is there an angry god up in the sky wreaking havoc on this planet as a form of punishment? Or are we being manipulated into doing these things that harm the life around us? In exploring the possibility that we are being manipulated, we know this can be done through the electromagnetic field. But looking deeper, we have to wonder if we have been designed to accept the programming of an authority, leaving us vulnerable to manipulation to cause harm. Much like AI is currently being programmed to do our bidding, maybe our species was once programmed to serve our masters.

The Mayan Popol Vuh tells us the gods wanted to make man to "nourish and sustain" them, and the Babylonian Enuma Elish tells us man was created as a slave race for the gods – should it come as a surprise then, that mankind is so easily manipulated given they were designed for a life of servitude? Furthermore, is it surprising that mankind willingly submits to the will of an authority? It would seem that our species instinctually desires to be ruled and finds comfort in being herded. We can easily turn a blind eye of ignorance on the massive amounts of suffering in the world. Are we that careless? Or is there a different mechanism at work that allows for our permission of suffering in the world?

"Let us make him who shall nourish and sustain us! What shall we do to be invoked, in order to be remembered on earth? We have already tried with our first creations, our first creatures; but we could not make them praise and venerate us. So, then, let us try to make obedient, respectful beings who will nourish and sustain us."[49]

If we look to the Babylonian creation myth known as the Enuma Elish, we see that Marduk, after defeating the goddess Tiamat, commanded Ea to create man "on whom the toil of the gods will be laid so they may rest," (Tablet VI line 8) ultimately creating man into a life of servitude to the gods in assisting them with their tasks.

Are we pre-programmed to accept hardship and other Loosh-producing events in our lives? We may sometimes fall victim to these terrible energies, but we may also be responsible for generating them. Our beliefs and our passions can blind us to the harm we may be causing, and our fears can motivate us to acts of cruelty. Whether we are targeting racial groups for discrimination, shouting insults at political rivals, or protesting one of the infinite causes that seem to spring up regularly, we have to recognize that we may be contributing to the problem. We may be spreading the toxic flow of energy that infects others and amplifies the issue

---

[49] English version by Delia Goetz and Sylvanus G. Morley from the Spanish translation by Adrián Recinos. (1950). Popol vuh : the sacred book of the ancient Quiché Maya. Norman :University of Oklahoma Press.

and produces more Loosh. But if we become mindful of our energetic output, we may be inclined to make different choices. If we are aware of the programming being thrown at us, we may have more strength to enact countermeasures. But if we continue to allow ourselves to remain in a state of ignorance, then we leave ourselves wide open and vulnerable to forces well-aware of the open energetic doorway to influence and manipulate human thoughts, behaviors, and actions.

Obedience

In 1963, Stanley Milgram, a psychologist at Yale University, conducted what became a very powerful experiment into the extremes of human obedience. His goal was to understand how so many Nazi soldiers were able to torture and execute millions of people simply because they were "following orders." In his experiment, the participants included a student, teacher, and an observer. The teacher watched as the student was connected to various wires and electrodes on one side of a wall. The teacher was then moved to another room on the other side of the wall where he was instructed to ask the student various questions. Whenever the student got the questions wrong, the teacher had to administer an electric shock, and the shocks grew in intensity with each wrong answer ranging from 15 volts to 450 volts. Despite the screams and pleas of the student, every-single-teacher administered a shock that would be harmful to human health (300 volts), and 65% of all teachers in the experiment administered lethal shocks (450 volts) to the students, despite their cries, and eventual silence on the other side of the wall. When the teachers questioned the observer and asked if they could stop the experiment, the observer simply informed them they needed to continue with the experiment. Unbeknownst to the teachers, however, the "students" were actually a part of the experiment and not really being harmed.[50]

The results of this experiment were shocking, and offered an insight into the darkness of human potential. It demonstrated the weakness of the human spirit to succumb to a perceived authority, no matter what the costs. In 1974, Milgram discussed his Agency Theory, which states that when in social

---

[50] McLeod, S (2017). The Milgram Experiment. Retrieved from https://www.simplypsychology.org/milgram.html

situations, people have two states of behavior. The first state is known as the Autonomous State where people are in charge of and aware of their own actions. They are responsible for their behavior and take responsibility for it. The second state of behavior is the Agentic State where people allow their actions to be directed by others and pass the responsibility or blame for the consequences of those actions to the person directing their actions.[50]

What the Milgram experiment teaches us is that when certain conditions are met, people can be manipulated to do terrible things to include the torture and murder of another even if such actions go against their own moral compass. In order to place a person in the agentic state, however, two conditions must be met:

1. "The person giving the orders is perceived as qualified to direct other people's behavior. That is, they are seen as legitimate."[50]

2. "The person being ordered about is able to believe that the authority will accept responsibility for what happens."[50]

This may partially explain why members of

the military are able to engage in warfare and commit acts of violence against their perceived enemies, even if those enemies are embedded amongst women and children. Soldiers follow orders from a perceived qualified authority that will accept responsibility for the orders given. Therefore, a soldier is able to bypass his own moral values and act as an agent for the authority. When in the agentic state, as is the norm for soldiers in the military, it would be quite easy to manipulate the actions of entire armies to perform tasks lucrative for Loosh production.

It's important to note that this experiment was conducted several times with slight variations. As a result, Milgram was able to identify which factors affected obedience. These conditions were summarized in the Simply Psychology article as follows:

1. Uniform, where the experimenter dressed in a lab coat was called away at the beginning of the session and replaced by an ordinary civilian. When this happened, obedience dropped to 20%.[50]

2. Change of location – when the experiment location was moved from Yale to a run-

down office, obedience dropped to 47.5%.[50]

3. Two-Teacher Condition – when participants instructed the teachers to press the switches, obedience increased to 92.5%.[50]

4. Touch-Proximity Condition – when the teacher had to force the learners hand down onto a shock plate, obedience fell to 30%. This suggests that when participants aren't buffered from the consequences of their actions they may be less likely to perform harmful acts. (Is this why it's so easy to kill using drones?)[50]

5. Social Support Condition- when two other participants posing as teachers refused to obey, having one stop at 150 volts and the other at 210 volts, obedience fell to 10%.[50]

6. Absent Experimenter Condition – when the experimenter instructed and prompted the teacher by telephone from another room, obedience fell to 20.5%.[50]

In considering the possibility that our species is being manipulated to create conditions of suffering in order to produce Loosh, this information can prove to be incredibly valuable. We need to be mindful of our vulnerabilities to manipulation. We also need to instill our own internal psychological defense mechanisms and question difficult orders that may come down from authority figures – whether we are soldiers in battle or insurance associates pushing a potentially detrimental policy that will negatively impact clients. We have the power to resist the manipulation. As the social support condition shows us, when others are refusing to obey, others will follow! Resistance will not always be easy, especially if optimal conditions for the agentic state supported by fearful consequences are in place. The perceived authority permeates our society and allows for the continued suffering of life on this planet. In looking at the design of life, it's easy to argue that animals are meant to be eaten because (God, nature, etc.) designed it to be that way. We can then transfer blame onto the authority of God or Nature and no longer be concerned about sending animals to the slaughterhouse because it's not our choice. What happens when we question the unquestionable - when we evaluate the benefits of God's plan or Nature's design? What happens when we examine the intentions of those authorities and find our best-interests aren't always served. Do we continue to follow orders, or do we try something different?

We need to listen to our own internal moral authorities if we are to enact change. We need to be willing to face the consequences of disobedience if we are to empower the positive flow of energy in our surrounding communities. We now understand that we have an energetic connection to everything around us. We have the power to influence that field through our thoughts, feelings, and actions, and ultimately promote peace. We need to be mindful and aware of the agentic state and do our best to operate in the autonomous state, taking responsibility for our actions and being mindful of the consequences of our actions or inactions.

But why were so many people so willing to give away their power at the expense of harming another simply because a random authority told them to do so? Why are so many of us willing to allow the terrible suffering of animals we use for food simply because an authority tells us it's okay? We have the power to say no, but willingly accept the programming of the authority because it's easier than forming a resistance. Submission is easier than standing out.

In a more-recent experiment that went viral on the Internet, a study was conducted in a waiting room demonstrating the programmability of people. In the beginning, all people in the waiting room were willing participants in the experiment. They were told to stand up whenever a bell rang in the room. Then, a subject unfamiliar with the experiment entered the room and sat down. When the bell rang, the entire room stood except for the subject. It only took a few moments before the new subject began standing at the toll of each bell. Eventually, all of the other volunteers were called out of the room, leaving the subject alone. The bell continued to ring, and she continued to stand. Furthermore, more unknowing subjects entered the room, and thanks to the conditioning of the initial subject, all new subjects also began standing whenever the bell rang.

But what would have happened if one of the subjects in the room refused to stand during the bell's ringing? What if they would have voiced the stupidity of the exercise without explanation? Experience tells us that most likely, one person's resistance would empower others to take a stand (or in this case seat), and stop the senseless activity. How many bells do you respond to in a given day?

The Power of Revolution

A few months ago, I was assigned to report to training during a teacher in-service day. It was scheduled to be an hour long and we were to meet in the auditorium at noon. When I arrived, there was a group of about 20 teachers patiently waiting for the administrators to arrive. We sat there making small talk, bored and joking about all of the other things we could (and should have) been doing. After about 5 minutes, another teacher informed us that the administrators had just left the building to get lunch, and would probably be gone for about an hour. The room remained relatively quiet, and people stayed in their seats. Someone asked: "should we leave?" but nobody responded. The unspoken consensus seemed to be to wait in the room until the administrators returned, despite knowing there'd be an extended, unplanned wait period. Knowing this was a complete waste of my time, and the consequences for leaving would probably be a simple announcement calling for us to return, I stood up laughing. "Are we really going to sit here for an hour with nothing to do?" I asked. "I'm leaving," I said with a smirk, and I began walking down the aisle. Immediately, just about everyone in the group stood up and followed. My simple rebellion had broken the programming, and we all experienced freedom from our fear of authority. Sometimes a simple act of defiance based on our own moral compass is all it takes to start a ripple effect that will counteract our internal programming and external influences.

Although we may have a tendency, or even a programmability to follow authority blindly, we also possess the power to think for ourselves and act independently from authority. We have to power to take a stand and ignore things that violate our own moral and conscious code. We simply need the willpower and courage to follow those instincts and start contributing to the world we want to see.

A Future Model for a Peaceful Society

When I first started writing this book, I was angry and I was afraid. I had just witnessed the slow, torturous death of my father and my world was completely shattered. I had glimpsed the other side and realized that there were forces at work that created and then preyed on human suffering. The safety of my false perception of reality had been rapidly dismantled as life and death were presented to me in a new light. I came to view human life as a food source for our predators, and realized that everyone I cared about – everyone on the entire planet – were no different than the factory-farm animals corralled into tiny containers forced to suffer the screams of their dying brethren as they were made into varying delicacies to satisfy humanities unending hunger. We are all cattle, and the farmers care little for our cries of pain and suffering.

This book was initially meant to be a work of despair – a desperate cry for help in a hopeless world filled with suffering and hardship. But something happened as I began working on this project. As I set out to prove that energy parasites exist and are feeding off of us, I first tried to find evidence of the existence of our own fields of energy that served as their food source. As you have already read, thanks to the research and testimony of others, I found several examples of the human energy field: our 6th sense, Castenada's glowing coat of awareness, and Strieber's electromagnetic sense organ. Source after source, I found examples of this field. I found it exists in plants, thanks to the work of Cleve Backster, which led me to believe that this field is universal and we are all connected and conscious. The HeartMath research further demonstrated the power of this field through studies proving the empathetic communication through the heart's electromagnetic field. What I learned in my search to validate my fears of hopelessness and predation was that we are in fact NOT powerless and therefore have hope!

Our electromagnetic field is a part of our essence – it is our life force and our connection to this universe. It is through this field that we have the ability to heal. Through techniques like Reiki, we can heal ourselves and we can heal one-another. We can also use this field to learn and gather information. With procedures like remote viewing we can collect verifiable data to help us navigate the many challenges life throws our way. With Robert Monroe's out-of-body techniques, we can travel the universe, explore alien landscapes, and access a wealth of knowledge to learn about ourselves and our existence. But we first must recognize this field exists and is connected through each one of us. We can use this field, and we must, but it is going to take some work.

Presently, our energetic field contains dangerous toxins that have contaminated our species, making us sick and ignorant. We are fish in a polluted ocean, in desperate need of decontamination. But this cleansing won't come from a benevolent god or helpful alien race. It must come from us! The Maharishi Affect has demonstrated that just a tiny amount of meditators can influence this field and impact the behaviors of a larger community. One percent is all that is needed to make a change. That change can start with you! The Milgram Experiment has shown us that most people are willing to perform harmful tasks against others if a perceived authority tells them to do so. Everywhere we look, authorities are telling us its okay to continue living our lives in this fashion that is detrimental to the planet, so our species continues on this destructive path. The media floods our minds with fear, forcing us to focus on surviving instead of thriving in this world of beautiful potential. But what if a small number of us stood up and tried something different? What if we looked instead to the authority within ourselves that silently screams at the insanity of unnecessary suffering and decided to make a change? Instead of fighting the perceived opposition, what if we were able to change the energetic influence surrounding them and cleanse the negativity from their own respective fields? What if such a cleansing would allow for them to heal and the need for "fighting the opposition" went away without confrontation? Such a change may not be as difficult as it may sound.

If you are reading this book, then you have

the potential to be a part of the change the world needs. You have the potential to bring healing to a world that so desperately craves it. You can be the change, but your first must make the choice to recognize it is needed.

I envision a world where schools teach meditation and mindfulness. They empower our children to look within and find inner peace. They teach our children to access their 6th sense and rely on it as we do our other 5 senses. These schools have better grades, lower discipline, and build communities of service-oriented citizens focused on improving the world without destruction and suffering.

I envision a world where we are open to utilizing remote viewing data. In following the Farsight Institutes TimeCross project where they are predicting the news every month, one month in advance, I envision a world where every single township and community employs a team of viewers. Their task would be to focus on major events that will impact their communities. Since the target areas will be known, specific, and small, analysts will be able to better utilize that data to take corrective or preventative measures. Death tolls from natural disasters can be drastically reduced, terrorist attacks can be prevented, lives can be saved and peace & happiness can be maintained.

I envision a world where every township and community employs a team of meditators totaling at least 1% of the target population. Their role would be to focus on the energetic frequencies in their communities and work to convert them from negative to positive. I envision every community working to improve the energetic interactions throughout the world to bring the much-needed peace and change to this world.

I envision a world where energy healing is employed as regularly as pharmaceuticals, and practitioners work to treat our energetic bodies as well as our physical ones. I envision practitioners bringing comfort to those who are ill, and peace & understanding to those who are dying. I envision energy workers clearing patients of all energetic parasites.

I envision a world where science is open to spiritual principals, even if they cannot yet be measured. I envision further exploration of this universe and our connection to other parallel worlds. I envision humanity learning to travel between worlds to learn from others through out-of-body states.

I envision a world that embraces our true history and teaches us about who we truly are. I envision us learning of the external influences, the manipulations, and our failures as a society to promote growth and peace. I envision humanity evolving from this knowledge and breaking the cycle of repetition and suffering.

I envision a world where we have learned to live in balance and harmony. We have eliminated suffering on this planet, and obtain our food through peaceful means. We are mindful of the energetic influence, and if slaughter is necessary, find a way to ensure the life we consume is afforded a beautiful life until the moment of death, which will be a quick, respectful, and peaceful transition.

I envision that you, the reader of this book, are a part of this transition and my words have inspired you to be this change. I envision this change starting right now and spreading throughout society, so that one-day we all will find peace.

I envision that when we create such a world,

our energetic parasites will no longer find sustenance from us and will be forced to leave this world or face starvation.

This is my vision. This is my hope. This is my reality.

Dad

My father died. His death was horrible, but that death does not define his legacy. My father was a wonderful, caring man filled with humor, love for his family, and compassion. When I think of him, which I do often, I am filled with joy. As a parent, I see my father's legacy living within me, and thriving in my children. I can hear him in my own voice when I face the challenges of parenthood. My son is so much like me: high energy and full of life. At times I grow frustrated with his constant movement and chatter and find myself wanting to scream out in anger. In those moments, I think about how my father handled such situations and I remember his humor. He was always quick with a sarcastic comment or silly game to redirect our energy. He was quick to make us laugh. Now that I am in that position, I recognize the power and beauty of such an approach. Parenthood is hard and frustrating at times, but instead of contributing to the negative flow of energy within our home, my father often found a way to convert his energy of frustration to an energy of love and laughter. For that, I am grateful, as it has become one of my greatest tools not only as a parent, but as a member of the human species. We can convert the negativity into something positive and avoid long gazes into the abyss of negativity.

Looking Beyond the Suffering

Dad's death was a horrible experience, and I am now faced with the realization that one of my greatest lessons in life about our own existence has come with a price tag I could not afford. Because my father died in the way he did, I have been forced to grow in ways I don't think would have been possible had it not happened. Because of the growth his death inspired, I have to come back to my thoughts on the purpose of our life and the enactment of suffering. Looking beyond the predation and parasitism that exists in all corners of this world, I have to wonder if there is a reason beyond survival for our suffering. I have to wonder if our Loosh-driven parasites hold a higher purpose that even they are unaware of in the universal program of evolution.

Without conflict, there would be no inspiration for growth and change. Without conflict, we would not evolve beyond our current state because we'd lack the motivation to do so. I often wish for an existence that lacks suffering and hardship. I wish for a world without the senseless suffering of life. But I wonder: could such a world survive? Would such a world evolve? Maybe to be truly free, we need to begin our lives as a blank program, fighting our way through the evolutionary and growth processes, ascending through the varying levels of aeons as we make our way towards the Pleroma. We'd need to acquire knowledge on our own through our personal experiences and internal processes so we can grow into the beings we choose to be. Then, we'd be free to create the utopia we've been searching for and have the experience to understand just how to manifest that reality. Through a deep reflection of our struggles and hardship, my hope is that we find peace, meaning, and value.

We can choose to focus on the possibility that we are infected with energetic parasites who consume our energy and manipulate our lives into a world of pain and suffering, or we can choose to empower ourselves through our own choices and mindful actions to enrich our lives and those of the people around us. If we really are food for the Archons, then choosing to fight amongst ourselves and even against our oppressors will only beget more suffering and yield higher Loosh production as we become the monsters we are fighting. However, by making the best of what may seem like a hopeless situation; by choosing to spread love and joy over fear, we may find happiness. And in that process of creating happiness, we may in-fact be creating a reality that is not suitable for those who wish to consume us...

We, those whom you see here, are, then, the avengers of the torments and suffering of our fathers.

Oj K'u paq'ol re wa'e ki ra'il, Ki k axk'ol ri qa qajaw.

~Mayan Popol Vuh

Acknowledgments

If my father didn't suffer, then this project would not have been possible. His death thrust me onto a path I was not prepared for, and I would trade all that I learned to have him back. I remember my father as a man dedicated to his family and madly in love with my mother. His sarcasm, diffusing humor and the family values he created will forever be his legacy. I remember my father not by the tragic way in which he died, but in the noble way in which he lived. I love you Dad and I work everyday to grow into the man you taught me to be. I love you Dad and I miss you ever-single-day.

To my wife Jenny and my children: this journey has not been easy for me, and as a result it's been hard on all of you. Thank you for continuing to love me through my anxiety, panic, anger, stress, and total confusion as I lost touch with reality and then fought to regain myself. I love you all so much.

To my mom Vicky and brother Michael: what we witnessed was pure hell, but we endured it together and for that I am thankful. We are Dads legacy and through us he lives on. Dad helped create something magical in our family, and that magic evolves through our new ventures yet serves to keep us bonded.

Aimee Wright, my cover artist and friend: Your artwork depicted *exactly* what this project needed. I am amazed at your ability to capture through a single image what took me over 50,000 words to express. You didn't miss a single element, and I am forever grateful for your support and attention to detail. You are an incredibly gifted artist and I know how hard you worked on this for me. Thank you so very much.

Ray Davis: You have been a voice of encouragement ever since I started this project. There were times when I felt like nobody cared and nobody wanted to listen yet there you were offering words of enthusiasm, encouragement, and excitement. You motivated me when I wanted to quit and encouraged me when I needed it most. The gift of your friendship helped this project to manifest, and I am incredibly thankful to call you a friend.

To my readers and listeners: Thank you! As an author, there is no greater feeling than knowing your work is appreciated, and for those of you who have reached out – your feedback has meant the world to me. Thank you for being a part of this journey with me.

Never Stop Questioning & Keep and Open Mind

Works Cited

1. Strieber, Whitley. (2011) *The Key: A True Encounter*. J.P. Tarcher/Penguin (pp.54)

2. Puthoff, Harold E. and Targ, Russel, (1976, March 3)"A Perceptional Channel for Information Transfer over Kilometer Distances: Historical Perspective and Recent Research." *Proceedings of the IEEE,* Vol. (pp. 64 329 – 354) Retrieved from http://www.espresearch.com/espgeneral/Remo te-Viewing-IEEE-1976.pdf

3. Brown, Courtney. (1996) Cosmic Voyage: a Scientific Discovery of Extraterrestrials Visiting Earth. Dutton. (pp. 16)

4. Monroe, Robert A. (1994) *Ultimate Journey*. Broadway Books.

5. Woolcott, I. (2018). Snake Power Animal Symbol Of Death Rebirth Eternity Mysteries Of Life Psychic Energy – Shamanic Journey. http://www.shamanicjourney.com/sn ake-power-animal-symbol-of-death-rebirth- eternity-mysteries-of-life-psychic-energy.

6. Eells, J. (2018). Cleve Backster Talked to Plants. And They Talked Back. The Lives They Lived.Retrieved from http://www.nytimes.com/news/the-lives-they- lived/2013/12/21/cleve-backster/

7. Backster, C. (1968). Evidence of Primary Perception in Plant Life. *The International Journal of Parapsychology.* Volume X, Winter 1968 Number 4. Retrieved at http://www.rebprotocol.net/clevebaxter/Evidence%20of% 20a%20Primary%20Perception%20In%20Plant%20Life %2023pp.pdf

8. Jensen,D (July 1997) The Plants Respond, An Interview with Cleve Backster. *The Sun.* Retrieved at https://www.thesunmagazine.org/issues/259/the-plants- respond

9. Braun, M; Kantor, P; Kleiner,B (Producers), & Green, W (Director). (1978). *The Secret Life of Plants.* Retrieved from https://www.youtube.com/watch?v=kTWcVnMPChM

10. McCraty, Rollin (2003). The Energetic Heart. Bioenergetic Interactions within and Between People. Bolder Creek, CA: Institute of HeartMath, (pp 1, 55, 9)

11. Ortega, X (2016, January). Lerina Garcia Gorda, The Woman from a Parallel Universe. Retrieved from http://www.ghosttheory.com/2016/01/12/lerina-garcia-gordo-the-woman-from-a-parallel-universe

12. Verochka, V. (2017, November). Philip K. Dick: Computer Programmed Reality. Retrieved from https://archive.org/details/PhilipKDickComputerProgrameredReality

13. Wachowski, L; "et al" (Producers), The Wachowski Brothers (Directors) (1999) The Matrix (Motion Picture), United States.

14. Bostrom, N. (2003) Are you Living in a Computer Simulation? Philosophical Quarterly Vol. 53, No 211 pp 243 – 255 (first version 2001)

15. Howe, L. M. (2016 December) Is Our Universe Someone Else's Computer Simulation? Retrieved from https://www.thehighersidechatsplus.com/forums/threads/linda-moulton-howe-our-universe-is-someone-elses-computer-simulation.7720/ *no longer available. Video transcription by Howe at https://www.youtube.com/watch?v=4FbD_ojWWXw by *Ozark Mountain Publishing*

16. Wootson, C. (2017 July 16). Elon Musk Doesn't Think We're Prepared to Face Humanities Biggest Threat: Artificial Intelligence. Retrieved from https://www.washingtonpost.com/news/innovations/wp/2017/07/16/elon-musk-doesnt-think-were-prepared-to-face-humanitys-biggest-threat-artificial-intelligence/?noredirect=on&utm_term=.f488eaeb0262

17. Knight, W. (2018 March 27). Fake News 2.0: Personalized, Optimized, and Even Harder to Stop. Retrieved from https://www.technologyreview.com/s/610635/fake-news-20-personalized-optimized-and-even-harder-to-stop/

18. McFarland, M. (2017 April 21) Elon Musks New Plan to Save Humanity from AI. Retrieved from https://money.cnn.com/2017/04/21/technology/elon-musk-brain-ai/index.html

19. Zeitchik, S. (2018 March 28). It could be the biggest change to movies since sound. If anyone will pay for it. Retrieved from https://www.washingtonpost.com/business/economy/it-could-be-the-biggest-change-to-movies-since-sound-if-anyone-will-pay-for-it/2018/03/28/ab9c7808-2f69-11e8-8688-e053ba58f1e4_story.html?noredirect=on&utm_term=.eb2a6ba4d514

20. Department of Physics – University of Maryland (accessed 2018 November 6) Gates, Sylvester College Park Professor Biography. Retrieved from https://umdphysics.umd.edu/people/faculty/current/item/167-gatess.html#biography

21. American Museum of Natural History. (2016 November 23). *Isaac Asamov Memorial Debate: The Theory of Everything.* (Video File) Retrieved From https://www.youtube.com/watch?v=Eb8_3BUHcuw

22. Pagels, E. H. (2007) The Nag Hammadi Scriptures. *Introduction* (pp 6 - 8) M. Meyer (Editor) New York, NY. HarperCollins Publishers.

23. Turner, J.D. (2007) The Nag Hammadi Scriptures. *Zostrianos* (pp. 537 – 588). M. Meyer (Editor) New York, NY. HarperCollins Publishers.

24. Meyer, M. (2007) The Nag Hammadi Scriptures. *On The Origin of the World (pp 203).* M. Meyer (Editor). New York, NY. HarperCollins Publishers.

25. Nash, John L. (2006 October). Not In His Image (pp 159). White River Junction, VT, Chelsea Green Publishing.

26. The Editors of Encyclopaedia Britannica (2015 December 24) Encyclopaedia Britannica. *Aeon.* Encyclopaedia Britannica, Inc. Retrieved from https://www.britannica.com/topic/aeon

27. Kubrick, S; "et al" (Producers), Kubric, S, (Director) (1987) Full Metal Jacket (Motion Picture), United States

28. Yong, E. (2013, November 6) Trees Trap Ants into Sweet Servitude. Retrieved from http://news.nationalgeographic.com/news/2013/11/131106-ants-tree-acacia-food-mutualism/

29. Gammon, K. (2012, September 7). *Zombie Bugs: 5 Real Life Cases of Body Snatching.* Retrieved from https://www.livescience.com/34196-zombie-animals.html

30. Centers for Disease Control and Prevention (2018, September 5). *Parasites – Toxoplasmosis (Toxoplasma Infection)* Retreived from https://www.cdc.gov/parasites/toxoplasmosis/biology.html

31. Bedroy, M., Webster, J., & Macdonald, D. (1998, October 10). Fatal Attraction in Rats Infected with Toxoplasma Gondii. *The Royal Society* (PDF) Retreived from https://www.ncbi.nlm.nih.gov/pmc/articles/PMC1690701/pdf/11007336.pdf

32. Karolinska Institutet (2012, December 6). How Common 'Cat Parasite' Gets into Human Brain and Influences Human Behavior. *ScienceDaily* Retreived From https://www.sciencedaily.com/releases/2012/12/121206203240.htm

33. Reiber, C. Et. Al. (2010, October 20). Change in Human Social Behavior in Response to Common Vaccine. *Annals of Epidemiology* Retreived from https://www.ncbi.nlm.nih.gov/pubmed/20816312

34. Icke, David (1999, February) The Biggest Secret. Isle of Wight, UK: David Icke Books

35. Castaneda, Carlos (1998) The Active Side of Infinity (pp 219 – 221). New York, NY: Laugan Productions.

36. Meyer, Marvin (2007) The Nag Hammadi Scriptures. *The Nature of the Rulers* (pp 187 – 198)

37. Goetz, D, Morley, S.G. (translated) Popul Vuh. Retrieved from https://archive.org/stream/PopolVuh/1019117-The-Popol-Vuh-English_djvu.txt

38. Nietzche, F. (2002) Beyond Good and Evil. (PDF) New York, NY, Cambridge University Press. Retrieved from https://www.holybooks.com/wp-content/uploads/Nietzsche-Beyond-Good-and-Evil.pdf

39. King, M.L. (1963) Strength to Love.

40. Dillbeck, M.C., Landrith, G., Orme-Johnson, D.W. (1981) Transcendental Meditation Program and Crime Rate change in a Sample of Forty-Eight Cities. *Journal of Criminal Justice, Volume 4 (pp 25 – 45)* Retrieved from https://www.ncjrs.gov/App/Publications/abstract.aspx?ID=85219

41. Medleson, Tamar, Et al. (May 2010) Feasibility and Preliminary Outcomes of a School-Based Mindfulness Intervention for Urban Youth. *Journal of Abnormal Child Psychology* 38(7):985 – 984. Doi: 10.1007/s10802-010-9418-x

42. St. George, Donna (2016, November 13) How Mindfulness Practices are Changing an Inner-City School. Retrieved from https://www.washingtonpost.com/local/education/how-mindfulness-practices-are-changing-an-inner-city-school/2016/11/13/7b4a274a-a833-11e6-ba59-a7d93165c6d4_story.html?noredirect=on&utm_term=.62a4ab90bd9a

43. Loos, H. G. (2001, June 1) Nervous system manipulation by electromagnetic fields from monitors. United States Patent 6,506,148. Retrieved from http://patft.uspto.gov/netacgi/nph-Parser?Sect1=PTO1&Sect2=HITOFF&d=PALL&p=1&u=%2Fnetahtml%2FPTO%2Fsrchnum.htm&r=1&f=G&l=50&s1=6506148.PN.&OS=PN/6506148&RS=PN/6506148

44. Loos, H.G. (1998, July 21) Method and apparatus for manipulating nervous system. United States Patent 5,782,874. Retrieved from http://patft.uspto.gov/netacgi/nph-Parser?Sect1=PTO1&Sect2=HITOFF&d=PALL&p=1&u=%2Fnetahtml%2FPTO%2Fsrchnum.htm&r=1&f=G&l=50&s1=6506148.PN.&OS=PN/6506148&RS=PN/5782874

45. English version by Delia Goetz and Sylvanus G. Morley from the Spanish translation by Adrián Recinos. (1950). Popol vuh : the sacred book of the ancient Quiché Maya. Norman :University of Oklahoma Press.

46. McLeod, S (2017). The Milgram Experiment. Retrieved from https://www.simplypsychology.org/milgram.html

I Am Human

&

We Are Not Who We Think We Are...

Read book 1 in the *I Am Human* series FREE!

"This author's realization that fear is the bottom line of our lives is profound, and through his writing, one feels the desperation and sense of panic this realization engenders.

His deep faith in the existence of "genuine good" sustains his journey from profound despair to his determination to find a way out of the life/death trap in which we've been ensnared. His realization that "Reality is not Real" is a profound turning point, and his references to the movie, The Matrix, were helpful in illustrating his points."

~ Deborah Kane

https://www.6SenseMedia.net/IAMHuman

"Be the change, never stop questioning & keep an open mind…"

A weekly podcast for TruthSeikers examining reality and our role in it. Available on SoundCloud, iTunes, and at:

https://www.6SenseMedia.net

Service of Change

A free newsletter for TruthSeikers. Get informed & stay connected on our search for Truth and Knowledge!

We are not a fear-based platform! ☺

Made in the USA
San Bernardino, CA
06 July 2020